Contents

Introduction

Chapter activities

Answers to chapter activities

Practice assessments

Answers to practice assessments

Also available from Osborne Books...

Tutorials

Clear, explanatory books written
precisely to the specifications

Wise Guides

Handy pocket-sized study and revision guides

Student Zone

Login to access your free ebooks and
interactive revision crosswords

Download **Osborne Books App** free from the App Store or Google Play Store
to view your ebooks online or offline on your mobile or tablet.

www.osbornebooks.co.uk

Management Accounting: Costing

Workbook

David Cox

Published by Osborne Books Limited
Email books@osbornebooks.co.uk
Website www.osbornebooks.co.uk

Design by Laura Ingham

Printed by CPI Group (UK) Limited, Croydon, CR0 4YY, on environmentally friendly, acid-free paper from managed forests.

MIX
Paper from
responsible sources
FSC® C019777
FSC
www.fsc.org

British Library Cataloguing in Publication Data
A catalogue record for this book is available from the British Library

ISBN 978 1909173 767

Introduction

Qualifications covered

This book has been written specifically to cover the Unit 'Management Accounting: Costing' which is a mandatory Unit for the following qualifications:

AAT Advanced Diploma in Accounting – Level 3

AAT Advanced Certificate in Bookkeeping – Level 3

AAT Advanced Diploma in Accounting at SCQF – Level 6

This book contains Chapter Activities which provide extra practice material in addition to the activities included in the Osborne Books Tutorial text, and Practice Assessments to prepare the student for the computer based assessments. The latter are based directly on the structure, style and content of the sample assessment material provided by the AAT at www.aat.org.uk.

Suggested answers to the Chapter Activities and Practice Assessments are set out in this book.

Osborne Study and Revision Materials

The materials featured on the previous page are tailored to the needs of students studying this Unit and revising for the assessment. They include:

- **Tutorials:** paperback books with practice activities
- **Wise Guides:** pocket-sized spiral bound revision cards
- **Student Zone:** access to Osborne Books online resources
- **Osborne Books App:** Osborne Books ebooks for mobiles and tablets

Visit www.osbornebooks.co.uk for details of study and revision resources and access to online material.

Chapter activities

1   An introduction to cost accounting

1.1   Which of the following statements describe features of financial accounting and which describe features of cost accounting?

Statement	Financial accounting	Cost accounting
Reports relate to what has happened in the past		
May be required by law		
Gives estimates of costs and income for the future		
May be made public		
Gives up-to-date reports which can be used for controlling the business		
Is used by people outside the business		
Is designed to meet the requirements of people inside the business		
Shows details of the expected costs of materials, labour and expenses		
Records accurate amounts, not estimates		

1.2   Which **one** of the following is normally classed as a fixed cost for a manufacturing business?

(a)	Rent of premises	
(b)	Boxes used to pack the product	
(c)	Telephone costs where a charge is made for each call	
(d)	Electricity metered to production machines	

1.3   Which **one** of the following is normally classed as a variable cost for a manufacturing business?

(a)	Salary of accountant	
(b)	Rent of premises	
(c)	Raw materials to make the product	
(d)	Insurance of machinery	

1.4   You work as an accounts assistant for Gold and Partners LLP, an accountancy practice, which has three offices in districts of the city. The offices are at Triangle, South Toynton and St Faiths. The accounting system has been set up to show costs, revenue and money invested for each of these three offices of the practice as separate segments.

The partners have requested details for each segment of costs and revenue for last year, and the amount of money invested in each segment at the end of the year.

The accounts supervisor asks you to deal with this request and you go to the accounts and extract the following information for last year:

	Triangle	South Toynton	St Faiths
	£000	£000	£000
Costs: materials	75	70	80
labour	550	650	730
expenses	82	69	89
Revenue	950	869	1,195
Money invested	750	900	1,150

The accounts supervisor asks you to present the information for the partners in the form of a report which shows the costs, profit, return on investment (to the nearest percentage point) and revenue for each segment (office) of the practice.

1.5 Classify the following costs:

		Fixed	Semi-variable	Variable
(a)	Rent of business premises			
(b)	Week's hire of machinery at £100 per week for one particular job			
(c)	Telephone system with a fixed line rental and a cost per call			
(d)	Supervisor's wages			
(e)	Diminishing (reducing) balance depreciation			
(f)	Production-line employees paid a basic wage, with a bonus linked to output			
(g)	Royalty paid to author for each book sold			
(h)	Accountant's fees			
(i)	Raw materials used in production			

1.6   Creative Clothing Limited manufactures clothes. You are to classify the company's costs into:

- direct materials
- indirect materials
- direct labour
- indirect labour
- direct expenses
- indirect expenses

The cost items to be classified are:

Cost item	Classification (write your answer)
Insurance of buildings	
Salaries of office staff	
Zip fasteners	
Electricity	
Wages of factory supervisors	
Pay of machine operators	
Consignment of blue denim cloth	
Stationery for the office	
Television advertising	
Oil for production machines	
Fuel for delivery vans	
Wages of canteen staff	

If you believe alternative classifications exist, argue the case and state if you need further information from the company.

1.7 Bunbury Buildings Limited makes garages and garden sheds which are pre-fabricated as a 'flat pack' in the factory to customer specifications

You are working in the costing section of Bunbury Buildings Limited and are asked to analyse the following cost items into the appropriate column and to agree the totals:

Cost item	Total cost £	Prime cost £	Production overhead costs £	Admin- istration costs £	Selling and distribution £
Wages of employees working on pre-fabrication line	19,205				
Supervisors' salaries	5,603				
Materials for making pre-fabricated panels	10,847				
Cleaning materials for factory machinery	315				
Sundry factory expenses	872				
Salaries of office staff	6,545				
Repairs to sales staff cars	731				
Depreciation of office equipment	200				
Magazine advertising	1,508				
Sundry office expenses	403				
Hire of display stands used at garden centres	500				
Office stationery	276				
TOTALS	47,005				

1.8　　Which **one** of the following describes the ethical principle of integrity?

(a)	Accounting staff should prepare cost accounting information without manipulation or bias	
(b)	Accounting staff are required to maintain their professional knowledge and skill to provide a competent service	
(c)	Accounting staff should not normally disclose confidential accounting information	
(d)	Accounting staff are straightforward and honest in all professional and business relationships	

2 Materials costs

2.1 You have the following information for boxes of 500 C5 envelopes:

- annual usage   200 boxes
- ordering cost   £30.00 per order
- inventory holding cost   £1.20 per box per year

What is the Economic Order Quantity (EOQ)?

(a)	25 boxes	
(b)	50 boxes	
(c)	100 boxes	
(d)	200 boxes	

2.2 Which **one** of these is an example of ethical behaviour by accounting staff in respect of inventory valuation?

(a)	Inventory is valued so as to maximise profits	
(b)	Inventory is valued in accordance with IAS2, *Inventories*	
(c)	Inventory is valued in a subjective way	
(d)	Inventory is valued using the basis decided by the business owner	

2.3   The supplies department of Peoples Bank has the following movements of an item of inventory for June 20-3:

		Units	Cost per unit £	Total cost £
1 June	Balance	2,000	2.00	4,000
15 June	Receipts	1,500	2.35	3,525
21 June	Issues	3,000		

You are to complete the following table for FIFO and AVCO:

Date 20-3	Description	FIFO £	AVCO £
21 June	Total issue value		
30 June	Total closing inventory value		

2.4   Wyezed Limited manufactures a product using two types of materials, Wye and Zed. The accounting policy of the company is to issue material Wye to production using the FIFO method, and material Zed on the AVCO method.

The following are the inventory movements of materials during the month of August 20-1:

Material Wye – FIFO method

20-1		Kilos (kg)	Cost per kg £
1 Aug	Balance	5,000	5.00
10 Aug	Receipts	2,000	5.25
18 Aug	Receipts	3,000	5.50
23 Aug	Issues	8,000	

Material Zed – AVCO method

20-1		Kilos (kg)	Cost per kg £
1 Aug	Balance	10,000	4.00
6 Aug	Receipts	5,000	4.30
19 Aug	Receipts	6,000	4.45
24 Aug	Issues	12,000	

You are to complete the inventory records on the next page, for material Wye and material Zed (showing the cost per kilogram to two decimal places).

INVENTORY RECORD: FIFO

Product: Material Wye

Date	Receipts			Issues			Balance		
20-1	Quantity (kg)	Cost per kg	Total Cost	Quantity (kg)	Cost per kg	Total Cost	Quantity (kg)	Cost per kg	Total Cost
	£	£		£	£		£	£	
1 Aug	Balance						5,000	5.00	25,000
10 Aug	2,000	5.25	10,500						
18 Aug	3,000	5.50	16,500						
23 Aug									

INVENTORY RECORD: AVCO

Product: Material Zed

Date	Receipts			Issues			Balance		
20-1	Quantity (kg)	Cost per kg	Total Cost	Quantity (kg)	Cost per kg	Total Cost	Quantity (kg)	Cost per kg	Total Cost
	£	£		£	£		£	£	
1 Aug	Balance						10,000	4.00	40,000
6 Aug	5,000	4.30	21,500						
19 Aug	6,000	4.45	26,700						
24 Aug									

2.5   Wyevale Tutorial College is a private college which runs courses for local companies on business and management subjects. The inventory records of photocopying paper are maintained on the FIFO method at present. The College's accountant has suggested that a change should be made to the AVCO method.

As an accounts assistant you have been asked to prepare information based on the movements of photocopying paper for February 20-8 which are as follows:

1 February	Opening inventory	100 reams* at £2.00 per ream
5 February	Issues	50 reams
10 February	Purchases	150 reams at £2.20 per ream
15 February	Issues	100 reams
18 February	Purchases	200 reams at £2.30 per ream
24 February	Issues	120 reams
		*a ream is 500 sheets

You are to:

(a)   Complete the inventory record on the next page for February, using the FIFO method.

(b)   Complete the inventory record on page 15 for February, using the AVCO method.

Show the costs per ream in £ to two decimal places.

(a)

INVENTORY RECORD: FIFO

Product: Photocopying paper (reams)

Date	Receipts			Issues			Balance		
20-8	Quantity (reams)	Cost per ream £	Total Cost £	Quantity (reams)	Cost per ream £	Total Cost £	Quantity (reams)	Cost per ream £	Total Cost £
1 Feb	Balance						100	2.00	200

(b)

INVENTORY RECORD: AVCO

Product: Photocopying paper (reams)

Date	Receipts			Issues			Balance		
20-8	Quantity (reams)	Cost per ream £	Total Cost £	Quantity (reams)	Cost per ream £	Total Cost £	Quantity (reams)	Cost per ream £	Total Cost £
1 Feb	Balance						100	2.00	200

2.6   SummerDaze Limited manufactures plastic garden furniture. Its best seller is the 'Calypso' seat made from white plastic.

The company uses the first in, first out (FIFO) method of issuing inventories.

As an accounts assistant at SummerDaze you have been given the following tasks:

Task 1

Complete the following inventory record for white plastic for April 20-9. Show the cost per kilogram to three decimal places and the total costs in whole £. Only one entry is permitted per inventory cell.

INVENTORY RECORD: FIFO

Product: White plastic

Date	Receipts			Issues			Balance	
	Quantity (kg)	Cost per kg £	Total Cost £	Quantity (kg)	Cost per kg £	Total Cost £	Quantity (kg)	Total Cost £
20-9								
Balance at 1 April							20,000	20,000
7 April	10,000	1.10	11,000				30,000	31,000
12 April				25,000				
20 April	20,000	1.20	24,000					
23 April				15,000				

Task 2

All issues of white plastic are for the manufacture of the 'Calypso' seat. The following cost accounting codes are used to record materials costs:

code number	description
2000	inventory – white plastic
2100	production – Calypso seats
3000	trade payables/purchases ledger control

Complete the following table to record the journal entries for the two purchases and two issues of white plastic in the cost accounting records.

20-9	Code number	Debit £	Credit £
7 April			
7 April			
12 April			
12 April			
20 April			
20 April			
23 April			
23 April			

2.7 The following information is available for metal grade X8:

- Annual demand – 36,125 kilograms
- Annual holding cost per kilogram – £3
- Fixed ordering cost – £30

(a) **You are to** calculate the Economic Order Quantity (EOQ) for X8.

> EOQ =   kg

The inventory record shown below for metal grade X8 for the month of May has only been fully completed for the first three weeks of the month.

(b) Complete the entries in the inventory record for the two receipts on 24 and 27 May that were ordered using the EOQ method.

(c) Complete ALL entries in the inventory record for the two issues in the month and for the closing balance at the end of May using the AVCO method of issuing inventory.

Show the costs per kilogram (kg) in £ to three decimal places, and the total costs in whole £. Only one entry is permitted per inventory cell.

Inventory record for metal grade X8

Date	Receipts			Issues			Balance	
	Quantity (kg)	Cost per kg £	Total Cost £	Quantity (kg)	Cost per kg £	Total Cost £	Quantity (kg)	Total Cost £
Balance as at 22 May							420	1,512
24 May		3.711						
26 May				900				
27 May		3.755						
30 May				800				

2.8   Harvie Ltd uses raw material HA24 in the manufacture of its products. The company had the following quantities of HA24 in inventory:

Date purchased	Quantity (kg)	Cost per kilo £	Total cost £
4 July	6,000	8.00	48,000
8 July	4,000	8.20	32,800
20 July	7,500	8.50	63,750

From the following amounts, insert the correct cost into the cost column of the table below to record the issue of 12,000 kg of HA24 on 21 July and to record the inventory balance after the issue using:

- FIFO (first in, first out)
- AVCO (weighted average cost)

Amounts:

£44,000	£96,000
£45,430	£97,800
£46,750	£99,120
£48,550	£100,550

	Cost
FIFO issue	
AVCO issue	
FIFO balance	
AVCO balance	

2.9 Indicate the statements which apply to the method(s) of inventory valuation. **Note:** statements may apply to more than one method.

Statement	FIFO	LIFO	AVCO
Issues from inventory are from the most recent receipts			
In times of rising prices, reported profits will usually be lower than with other methods			
Closing inventory is based on more recent costs of goods received			
Issues from inventory are from the earliest receipts			
Acceptable for tax purposes			
Closing inventory is valued at a weighted average cost			
Permitted by IAS 2, *Inventories*			
In times of rising prices, the cost of sales figure will usually be lower than with other methods			
Closing inventory is based on older costs of goods received			

3 Labour costs

3.1 Renne Limited pays its employees their basic pay at a time rate per hour, for a 35-hour week.

For any overtime in excess of 35 hours per week, the extra hours are paid at basic pay plus overtime. There are two overtime rates:

- rate 1: basic rate + one-third.

- rate 2: basic rate + 50%.

The details of three employees for last week are as follows:

Employee	Basic rate per hour	Basic hours	Overtime rate 1 (hours)	Overtime rate 2 (hours)
L Constantinou	£12.80	35	–	5
H Gunther	£15.00	35	2	1
J White	£10.20	35	5	2

Complete the table below to show the basic pay, overtime, and gross pay for the week.

Employee	Basic pay £	Overtime rate 1 £	Overtime rate 2 £	Gross pay for week £
L Constantinou				
H Gunther				
J White				

3.2   Elend Limited, a manufacturing company, pays its production-line employees on a piecework basis, but with a guaranteed time rate for the hours worked. The details of three employees for last week are as follows.

Employee	Time rate per hour	Hours worked	Production for week	Piecework rate
J Daniels	£12.00	38	800 units	55p per unit
L Ho	£11.50	35	650 units	65p per unit
T Turner	£11.75	36	500 units	90p per unit

Complete the table below to show the time rate, piecework rate, and the gross pay for the week.

Employee	Time rate £	Piecework rate £	Gross pay for week £
J Daniels			
L Ho			
T Turner			

3.3 Brock and Company, a manufacturing business, pays its production-line employees on a time basis. A bonus is paid where production is completed faster than the time allowed for a standard hour's production. The bonus is 50 per cent of the time saved and is paid at the time rate per hour. The details of four employees for last week are as follows:

Employee	Time rate per hour	Hours worked	Allowed per hour	Actual production
H Hands	£12.50	35	50 units	1,950 units
A Khan	£11.75	37	60 units	2,200 units
T Shah	£11.00	38	50 units	2,000 units
D Smith	£12.80	40	60 units	2,490 units

Note: there were no overtime payments last week.

Complete the table below to show the time rate, bonus (if any), and gross pay for the week.

Employee	Time rate £	Bonus £	Gross pay for week £
H Hands			
A Khan			
T Shah			
D Smith			

3.4   SummerDaze Limited manufactures plastic garden furniture. Its best seller is the 'Calypso' seat made from white plastic.

The payroll for the week ended 18 June 20-9 has been completed, with the following amounts to pay:

		£
•	net wages to be paid to employees	8,000
•	income tax and National Insurance Contributions (NIC) to be paid to HM Revenue & Customs	1,650
•	pension contributions to be paid to the pension fund	850
	PAYROLL FOR THE WEEK	10,500

The payroll for the week has been analysed as:

		£
•	direct labour costs	7,750
•	indirect labour costs	1,500
•	administration labour costs	1,250
		10,500

As an accounts assistant at SummerDaze you have been given the following tasks:

Task 1

Prepare the wages control account for the week ended 18 June 20-9:

Dr		Wages control account		Cr
	£			£

Task 2

All of the direct labour costs are for the manufacture of 'Calypso' seats. The following cost accounting codes are in use to record labour costs:

code number	description
2100	production – Calypso seats
2200	production overheads
2300	non-production overheads – administration
3100	wages control

Complete the table below to record the journal entries which show how the total cost of the payroll is split between the various cost centres of the business.

20-9	Code number	Debit £	Credit £
18 June	2100		
18 June	3100		
18 June	2200		
18 June	3100		
18 June	2300		
18 June	3100		

3.5   Perran Limited manufactures surf boards. The following data relates to the production of its 'Porth' brand of board for February 20-6:

Total direct labour hours worked	3,000 hours
Normal time hours	2,600 hours
Overtime hours	400 hours
Normal time rate	£10 per hour
Overtime rate	£15 per hour

In the company's cost bookkeeping system all direct labour overtime payments are included in direct costs.

The following cost accounting codes are in use to record labour costs:

code number	description
2100	production – 'Porth' boards
4400	wages control

(a)   Calculate the total cost of direct labour for February.

Total cost of direct labour for February:

(b)   State the cost bookkeeping entries, together with account codes, which will transfer the direct labour costs to production.

Account name	Account code	Debit £	Account name	Account code	Credit £

3.6 You are an accounts assistant at Cooper Limited and have been asked to help with calculating labour costs.

The cost accountant has given you the following time sheet for one of Cooper Limited's employees, S Patton, who is paid as follows:

- For a basic six-hour shift every day from Monday to Friday – basic pay

- For any overtime in excess of the basic six hours on any day from Monday to Friday – the extra hours are paid at time-and-a-half (basic pay plus an overtime premium equal to half of basic pay)

- For three contracted hours each Saturday morning – basic pay

- For any hours worked in excess of three hours on a Saturday or any hours worked on a Sunday – double-time (basic pay plus an overtime premium equal to basic pay)

You are to complete the time sheet columns headed basic pay, overtime premium and total pay (enter a zero figure, '0', in the columns where nothing is to be paid).

Note: overtime premium is just the premium paid for the extra hours worked.

Employee's weekly time sheet for week ending 11 August 20-8

Employee: S Patton			Profit Centre: Moulding			
Employee number: 617			Basic pay per hour: £12.00			
	Hours spent on production	**Hours worked on indirect work**	**Notes**	**Basic pay £**	**Overtime premium £**	**Total pay £**
Monday	6	0				
Tuesday	7	0				
Wednesday	6	2	10am-12noon training			
Thursday	8	0				
Friday	6	1	8am-9am maintenance			
Saturday	4	0				
Sunday	2	0				
Total	39	3				

3.7 Martley Manufacturing Limited pays some of its production employees on a piecework system, based on an agreed output per hour – standard hours produced – that they are allowed to manufacture components.

The following information relates to one of these employees last week:

Day	Actual hours worked	Standard hours produced
Monday	7	6
Tuesday	8	8
Wednesday	8	9
Thursday	9	11
Friday	8	7

The employee is paid £14 per standard hour produced.

You are to complete the sentences below by entering the correct figures:

(a) The employee's total pay for the week was £ [   ]

Now assume that the company offers a guaranteed minimum daily payment of £100.

(b) The employee's total pay for the week would now be £ [   ]

Now assume that, instead of a guaranteed minimum daily payment, the company offers a guaranteed minimum weekly payment of £550.

(c) The employee's total pay for the week would now be £ [   ]

Now assume that, instead of a guaranteed minimum weekly payment, the company pays for actual hours worked at the standard hour rate, together with a piecework bonus of £50.

(d) The employee's total pay for the week would now be £ [   ]

3.8   Scimitar Limited, a manufacturing business, has a Production Department where the employees work in teams. Their basic rate is £12.00 per hour and there are two rates of overtime as follows:

- Overtime rate 1: basic pay + 25%

- Overtime rate 2: basic pay + 50%

Scimitar Limited sets a target for production of every component each month. A team bonus equal to 10% of basic hourly rate is payable for every equivalent unit of production in the month in excess of the target.

The target for April was 6,000 units.

In April the production was 6,500 equivalent units.

All overtime and bonuses are included as part of the direct labour cost.

(a)   Complete the gaps in the table below to calculate the total labour cost.

Labour cost	Hours	£
Basic pay	320	
Overtime rate 1	25	
Overtime rate 2	25	
Total cost before team bonus	370	
Bonus payment		
Total cost including team bonus		

(b)   Calculate the total labour cost per equivalent unit of the finished production for April. Give your answer in £s to two decimal places.

The direct labour cost per equivalent unit for April is £ [   ]

Scimitar Limited has forecast the following information for the Production Department for May:

The basic hourly rate will be increased to £12.40 per hour. The target for production is still 6,000 units and the bonus, equal to 10% of basic hourly rate, is still payable for equivalent units of production in excess of this.

5,600 units will be completed in May and the closing work in progress is expected to be 1,000 units which will be 75% complete with regard to labour. No opening work in progress was expected at the start of May.

(c)   Complete the following sentence by filling in the blanks.

The equivalent units of production with regard to labour for May will be [   ]

and the bonus payable will be £ [   ]

3.9 Indicate the statements which apply to the method(s) of labour costs. **Note:** statements may apply to more than one method.

Statement	Time rate	Piecework rate	Bonus system
The gross pay calculation is: hours worked x rate per hour			
Method used for repetitive work where output is more important than quality			
The gross pay calculation is: gross pay + proportion of the time saved			
The employer has to set time allowances for work done			
Pay is not linked to output			
Employees can earn more by working harder			
There is no pressure on time, so quality of output should be maintained			
The amount earned by employees varies with output			
The gross pay calculation is: number of items produced x rate per item			

4 Overheads and expenses

4.1 Mereford Management College is a private college that has two teaching departments – accountancy and management.

The College charges overheads on the basis of teaching hours. The overhead analysis information which follows is available to you.

OVERHEAD ANALYSIS January 20-7		
	Accountancy Department	Management Department
Budgeted total overheads (£)	15,884	19,855
Budgeted teaching hours	722	1,045
Budgeted overhead absorption rate (£)		

You are to calculate the budgeted overhead absorption rate for each of the two departments.

Details of a particular course – 'Finance for Managers' – that is taught in both the accountancy and management departments are as follows:

OVERHEAD ANALYSIS Course: Finance for Managers		
	Accountancy Department	Management Department
Teaching hours	45	20
Budgeted overhead absorption rate (£)		
Overhead absorbed by course (£)		

You are to calculate the overhead absorbed by the 'Finance for Managers' course.

4.2   Wyevale Processing Limited processes and packs fruit and vegetables for supermarkets. The company has five departments – processing, packing, quality assurance, stores and maintenance.

The accounts supervisor has given you the budgeted production overhead schedule (see next page) to complete for next month.

The following information is available:

	Processing	Packing	Quality Assurance	Stores	Maintenance
Floor area (square metres)	160	210	50	80	100
Employees (number)	10	14	2	2	2
Equipment usage (hours)	300	100	40		

You are to complete the budgeted production overhead schedule for next month showing the basis of apportionment to the five departments of the business.

WYEVALE PROCESSING LIMITED
BUDGETED PRODUCTION OVERHEAD SCHEDULE
for next month

Budgeted overheads	Basis of apportionment	Totals £	Processing £	Packing £	Quality Assurance £	Stores £	Maintenance £
Rent and rates		4,500					
Supervisors' salaries		3,690					
Depreciation of equipment		2,640					
Canteen costs		720					
TOTAL		11,550					

4.3   Wyvern Private Hospital plc has two patient wards – a day care ward for minor operations where the patients go home at the end of the day, and a surgical ward for patients who remain in the hospital for several days. There are two service departments – the operating theatre and administration.

The overheads of each department for last month were as follows:

		£
•	day care ward	28,750
•	surgical ward	42,110
•	operating theatre	32,260
•	administration	9,075

The basis for re-apportioning the overheads of the service departments is:

• operating theatre, on the number of operations carried out – day care ward, 160; surgical ward, 120

• administration, on the number of staff in each department – day care ward, 10; surgical ward, 25; operating theatre, 20

You are to complete the table below, using the step-down method, to re-apportion the two service department overheads to the two patient wards.

Budgeted overheads	Day care ward £	Surgical ward £	Operating theatre £	Administration £	Totals £
Overheads					
Reapportion Administration					
Reapportion Operating theatre					
Total overheads to patient wards					

Another overhead is telephone and internet costs. The estimated cost for the next quarter is £9,500, which consists of a fixed element and a variable element. The fixed element is 30% of the total cost and the rest is variable. The fixed element of the total cost is to be apportioned between the day care ward and the surgical ward in the ratio 62:38. The variable element of the total cost is apportioned in the ratio of 72:28.

Complete the following sentences by inserting the correct values.

The fixed element of the telephone and internet costs that will be apportioned to the day care ward is:

£ _____

The variable element of the telephone and internet costs that will be apportioned to the surgical ward is:

£ _____

4.4 Milestone Motors Limited sells and services cars. The company's operations are organised into three profit centres and one support cost centre, as follows:

Profit centres

- New car sales
- Used car sales
- Servicing

Support cost centre

- Administration

The budgeted overheads of the company for the four weeks ended 28 April 20-2 are:

	£
Depreciation of non-current assets	8,400
Rent of premises	10,000
Other property overheads	4,500
Staff costs:	
– new car sales	11,080
– used car sales	7,390
– servicing	9,975
– administration	6,850
Administration overheads	3,860
Total	**62,055**

The following information is also relevant:

Profit/Cost centre	% of floor space occupied	Carrying amount of non-current assets
		£000
New car sales	40%	50
Used car sales	30%	30
Servicing	20%	100
Administration	10%	20
	100%	200

Overheads are allocated and apportioned using the most appropriate basis. The total administration overheads are then re-apportioned to the three profit centres using the following percentages.

- New car sales   20%
- Used car sales   30%
- Servicing   50%

Task 1

Complete the following table showing:

- the basis for allocation or apportionment of each overhead
- the allocation and apportionment of fixed overheads between the four centres
- the re-apportionment of the total administration overheads

Budgeted overheads for four weeks ended 28 April 20-2	Basis of apportion-ment	Totals £	New Car Sales £	Used Car Sales £	Servicing £	Administration £
Depreciation of non-current assets		8,400				
Rent of premises		10,000				
Other property overheads		4,500				
Staff costs		35,295				
Administration overheads		3,860				
		62,055				
Administration		62,055				

Task 2

Servicing centre overheads are absorbed on the basis of budgeted direct labour hours. The budgeted number of direct labour hours for the servicing centre during the four weeks ended 28 April 20-2 is 1,025 hours.

What is the budgeted overhead absorption rate per direct labour hour for the servicing centre during the period?

£ [   ] per direct labour hour

4.5 You work as an accounts assistant for Trujillo Limited, a manufacturing business. The company has two profit centres: cutting and assembly – and three support cost centres: maintenance, stores and administration.

Trujillo Limited's budgeted overheads for the next financial year are:

Budgeted overheads	£	£
Depreciation charge for machinery		4,200
Power for production		2,040
Rent and rates of premises		16,500
Light and heat for premises		12,750
Indirect labour costs:		
Maintenance	38,550	
Stores	29,850	
Administration	51,250	
Totals	119,650	35,490

The following information is also available:

Department	Carrying amount of machinery	Production power usage (KwH)	Floor space (square metres)	Number of employees
Profit centres:				
Cutting	100,000	15,000	600	4
Assembly	40,000	2,000	400	6
Support department cost centres:				
Maintenance			100	2
Stores			160	2
Administration			240	3
Total	140,000	17,000	1,500	17

Overheads are allocated or apportioned on the most appropriate basis. The total overheads of the support cost centres are then reapportioned to the two profit controo, uoing the direct method.

- 75% of the maintenance cost centre's time is spent maintaining machinery in the cutting profit centre and the remainder in the assembly profit centre.

- The stores cost centre makes 60% of its issues to the cutting profit centre and 40% to the assembly profit centre.

- Administration supports the two profit centres equally.

- There is no reciprocal servicing between the three support cost centres.

You are to complete the apportionment table below using the data above.

Budgeted overheads	Basis of apportionment	Cutting £	Assembly £	Maintenance £	Stores £	Admin £	Totals £
Depreciation charge for machinery							
Power for production							
Rent and rates of premises							
Light and heat for premises							
Indirect labour							
Totals							
Reapportion Maintenance							
Reapportion Stores							
Reapportion Administration							
Total overheads to profit centres							

4.6 Blenheim Limited's budgeted overheads and activity levels for the next quarter are:

	Moulding	Finishing
Budgeted overheads (£)	39,600	62,700
Budgeted direct labour hours	2,475	4,180
Budgeted machine hours	4,400	2,850

(1) What would be the budgeted overhead absorption rate for each department if this were set based on their both being heavily automated?

(a) Moulding £9 per hour; finishing £15 per hour	
(b) Moulding £16 per hour; finishing £22 per hour	
(c) Moulding £9 per hour; finishing £22 per hour	
(d) Moulding £16 per hour; finishing £15 per hour	

(2) What would be the budgeted overhead absorption rate for each department if this were set based on their both being labour intensive?

(a) Moulding £9 per hour; finishing £15 per hour	
(b) Moulding £16 per hour; finishing £22 per hour	
(c) Moulding £9 per hour; finishing £22 per hour	
(d) Moulding £16 per hour; finishing £15 per hour	

Additional data

At the end of the quarter actual overheads incurred were found to be:

	Moulding	Finishing
Actual overheads (£)	41,200	61,800

(3) Assuming that exactly the same amount of overheads were absorbed as budgeted, what were the budgeted under- or over-absorptions in the quarter?

(a)	Moulding over-absorbed £1,600; finishing over-absorbed £900	
(b)	Moulding over-absorbed £1,600; finishing under-absorbed £900	
(c)	Moulding under-absorbed £1,600; finishing under-absorbed £900	
(d)	Moulding under-absorbed £1,600; finishing over-absorbed £900	

4.7 Foregate Limited has the following budgeted information for the next quarter:

Budgeted overheads	£££,000
Direct labour hours	5,000
Direct labour cost	£62,500

(1) What is the budgeted overhead absorption rate using the direct labour percentage add-on method?

(a) 500 per cent	
(b) 20 per cent	
(c) 40 per cent	
(d) 250 per cent	

Additional data

At the end of the quarter actual direct labour hours were 5,500 and direct labour cost was £68,750.

(2) What is the amount of overhead that was absorbed in the quarter?

(a) £25,000	
(b) £27,500	
(c) £68,750	
(d) £5,500	

4.8 Garden Cottage Limited manufactures 'homestyle' soups which are sold through supermarkets and convenience stores. The soups pass through two departments – kitchen and canning. Details of overheads for the departments for the four weeks ended 16 June 20-6 are as follows:

Kitchen Department

- overhead absorption rate is £7.00 per direct labour hour
- direct labour hours worked were 800
- actual cost of production overhead was £5,000

Canning Department

- overhead absorption rate is £8.00 per machine hour
- machine hours worked were 400
- actual cost of production overhead was £3,500

The following cost accounting codes are in use to record overheads:

code number	description
2000	production
2100	production overheads: kitchen department
2200	production overheads: canning department
4000	statement of profit or loss

As an accounts assistant at Garden Cottage Limited, you are asked to prepare the two production overheads accounts and to fill in the table (on the next page) as at 16 June 20-6 to account for the overheads and the over- and under-absorption of overheads.

Dr	**Production Overheads Account: Kitchen Department (2100)**		Cr
	£		£

Dr	**Production Overheads Account: Canning Department (2200)**		Cr
	£		£

20-6	Code number	Debit £	Credit £

5 Methods of costing

5.1 OB Printers has been asked by John Dun, a local poet, to quote for the cost of printing a small book of poetry. John Dun is not sure how many copies to order and has asked for quotations for 500, 1,000 and 2,000 copies.

The estimates by OB Printers are as follows:

Setting up the printing machine:	6 hours at £10.00 per hour
Artwork:	7 hours at £12.00 per hour
Page setting:	20 hours at £15.00 per hour
Paper (for 500 copies):	£200.00
Other printing consumables (for 500 copies):	£100.00
Direct labour (for 500 copies):	5 hours at £13.00 per hour
Production overheads:	80% of direct labour costs
Profit:	25% of cost price

Task 1

Complete the Job Cost Sheet (see next page) for 500, 1,000 and 2,000 copies to show the estimated total cost of the job, and the selling price.

Task 2

Calculate the cost per book (to two decimal places) to the author at each of the three different production levels.

	Cost per book to author:
500 copies	£
1,000 copies	£
2,000 copies	£

JOB NO 12345

Poetry book for John Dun

	NUMBER OF COPIES		
	500	**1,000**	**2,000**
	£	£	£

Fixed Costs

Setting up machine

Artwork

Page setting

Direct Materials

Paper

Other printing consumables

Direct Labour

Production Overheads
(80% of direct labour costs)

TOTAL COST

Profit (25% of total cost)

SELLING PRICE

5.2   Chesford Limited, a manufacturing business, uses both batch and unit costing as appropriate in its Production Department. It is currently costing a new product, CH401 which will start production in batches of 15,000 units.

It has estimated that the following costs will be incurred in producing one batch of 15,000 units of CH401:

Product CH401 cost estimates	£ per batch
Direct materials	12,450
Direct labour	8,100
Variable overheads	6,450
Fixed production overheads	4,800
Administration, selling and distribution costs	4,200
Total costs	36,000

You are to

(a)   Calculate the prime cost of one unit of CH401.

£ [   ]

(b)   Calculate the full absorption cost of one unit of CH401.

£ [   ]

(c)   Calculate the marginal cost of one unit of CH401.

£ [   ]

(d)   Calculate the marginal production cost of one batch of CH401.

£ [   ]

(e)   Calculate the full absorption cost of one batch of CH401.

£ [   ]

(f)   Which **one** of the following costs will NEVER be included in Chesford Limited's inventory valuation?

(a)	Product costs	
(b)	Marginal costs	
(c)	Prime costs	
(d)	Period costs	

5.3   A manufacturer of security alarms has the following information concerning the first month of production:

Direct materials	£10,725
Direct labour	£6,600
Variable production overheads	£3,900
Security alarms completed	2,750
Security alarms in progress	500

The work-in-progress is complete as regards materials, but is 50% complete as regards direct labour and variable production overheads.

You are to complete the following layout to show the cost per security alarm (to two decimal places) of the first month's production and the month-end valuation for work-in-progress.

Cost element	Costs	Completed Units	Work-in-progress			Total	Cost	WIP
			Units	% complete	Equivalent Units	Equivalent Units	per Unit	valuation
	A	B	C	D	E	F	G	H
					C x D	B + E	A ÷ F	E x G
	£						£	£
Direct materials								
Direct labour								
Production overheads								
Total								

5.4   Wyvern Chemicals Limited produces a chemical, which is made in one production process.

For the four weeks ended 9 April 20-4, the company input 65,000 litres of direct materials, had an output of 60,000 litres and a normal loss of 5,000 litres. The input costs were: materials £19,500, labour £13,000, overheads £9,750. Normal losses were sold to a specialist reprocessing company for 5p per litre.

There was no opening or closing inventory at the beginning and end of the process; all output was complete.

(a)   As an accounts assistant, you are to complete the following process account for the four weeks ended 9 April 20-4.

Dr				Process Account			Cr
	Quantity (litres)	Unit cost	Total cost		Quantity (litres)	Unit cost	Total cost
		£	£			£	£
Materials				Normal loss			
Labour				Finished goods			
Overheads							

(b)   Identify the entry to be made in normal loss account.

	Debit £	Credit £
Normal loss		

5.5 Hawke Limited produces a washing powder called 'CleanO', which is made in one production process.

For the four weeks ended 24 September 20-3, the company input 84,000 kilos of direct materials, had an output of 81,000 kilos – the difference of 3,000 kilos was made up of a normal loss of 4,000 kilos and an abnormal gain of 1,000 kilos.

The input costs were: materials £16,800, labour £12,600, overheads £4,200. All losses were sold to a specialist reprocessing company for 20p per kilo.

There was no opening or closing inventory at the beginning and end of the process; all output was complete.

As an accounts assistant, you are to complete the following process account, the abnormal gain account and the normal loss account for the four weeks ended 24 September 20-3.

Dr				Process Account			Cr
	Quantity (kilos)	Unit cost £	Total cost £		Quantity (kilos)	Unit cost £	Total cost £
Materials				Normal loss			
Labour				Finished goods			
Overheads							
Abnormal gain							

Dr		Normal Loss Account		Cr
	£			£

Dr		Abnormal Gain Account		Cr
	£			£

5.6   Burncoose Limited is a manufacturer of vitamin tablets. Its best-selling product, called 'Vita' is made in two production processes before completion and transfer to finished goods.

For the four weeks ended 16 July 20-4, details of production of 'Vita' were as follows:

	Process 1	Process 2
Direct materials (5,000 kilos)	£2,000	–
Labour	£1,000	£1,125
Overheads	£500	£675
Normal loss in process	5% of input	3% of input
Output	4,500 kilos	4,400 kilos
Scrap value of all losses	£0.20 per kilo	£0.40 per kilo

There was no opening or closing inventory at the beginning and end of either process; all output was complete. All losses were sold to a specialist reprocessing company.

As an accounts assistant, you are to complete the following process 1 account and process 2 account for the four weeks ended 16 July 20-4. **Note:** show cost per unit of expected output to the nearest penny.

Dr				Process 1 Account			Cr
	Quantity (kilos)	Unit cost £	Total cost £		Quantity (kilos)	Unit cost £	Total cost £
Materials				Normal loss			
Labour				Transfer to			
Overheads				process 2			
				Abnormal loss			

Dr				Process 2 Account			Cr
	Quantity (kilos)	Unit cost £	Total cost £		Quantity (kilos)	Unit cost £	Total cost £
Transfer from process 1				Normal loss			
Labour				Finished goods			
Overheads							
Abnormal gain							

5.7   Zelah Chemicals Limited uses process costing for its products.

The process account for July for one particular process has been partly completed but the following information is also relevant:

- Four employees worked on this process during July. Each employee worked 35 hours per week for 4 weeks and was paid £12 per hour.

- Overheads are absorbed on the basis of £10 per labour hour.

- Zelah Chemicals Limited expects a normal loss of 5% during this process, which it then sells for scrap at 50p per kilo.

(a)   Complete the process account below for July.

Description	Kilos	Unit cost £	Total cost £	Description	Kilos	Unit cost £	Total cost £
Material ZC6	300	1.60		Normal loss		0.50	
Material ZC8	1,500	0.80		Output	1,900		
Material ZC10	200	1.50					
Labour							
Overheads							

(b)   Identify the correct entry for each of the following in a normal loss account.

	Debit	Credit
Process		
Abnormal gain		

6 Marginal, absorption and activity based costing

6.1 Outdoor Limited makes garden seats. The management of the company is considering the production for next year and has asked for help with certain financial decisions.

The following information is available:

Selling price (per seat)	£100	
Direct materials (per seat)	£25	
Direct labour (per seat)	£30	
Fixed production overheads	£100,000	per year
Non-production overheads	£50,000	per year

The company is planning to manufacture 4,000 seats next year.

You are to calculate:

- the marginal cost per seat
- the absorption cost per seat
- the profit or loss if 4,000 seats are sold

Complete the table below with your answers:

Marginal cost per seat	£
Absorption cost per seat	£
Profit or loss if 4,000 seats are sold	£

6.2   Strellis Limited manufactures one product, the Strell. For the month of June 20-5 the following information is available:

Number of units manufactured	4,000
Number of units sold	3,500
Selling price	£10 per unit
Direct materials for month	£10,000
Direct labour for month	£12,000
Fixed production overheads	£15,000 per month
Non-production overheads	£1,500 per month

There was no finished goods inventory at the start of the month. Both direct materials and direct labour are variable costs.

Required:

(a)   Produce statements of profit or loss for June 20-5, using:

   •   marginal costing
   •   absorption costing

(b)   Explain briefly the reason for the difference between recorded profits or losses under the alternative costing methods.

6.3   'Activity based costing has been developed as a development of absorption costing.'

(a)   Explain how activity based costing is used to calculate the cost of a product.

(b)   Explain two benefits of using activity based costing over using absorption costing.

6.4 CeeDee Limited makes two products, Cee and Dee. Product Cee is made in batches of 10,000 units, and Product Dee is made in batches of 1,000 units. Each batch has the following set-up and quality inspection costs:

- set-up £250

- quality inspection £150

Each week, the company produces 50,000 units of Cee and 50,000 units of Dee. At present the company charges overheads to output on the basis of labour hours, which are 500 hours per week for Cee and 500 hours for Dee.

Required:

(a) Calculate the overheads charged to Cee and Dee each week, on the basis of labour hours.

(b) Calculate the overheads charged to Cee and Dee each week, using activity based costing and the cost drivers of set-up and quality inspection.

(c) Advise the management of CeeDee Limited which is the more appropriate method of charging overheads to output.

6.5 Which **one** of these is an example of unethical behaviour by accounting staff?

(a)	Including product costs in the inventory valuation	
(b)	Using absorption costing for the inventory valuation	
(c)	Using FIFO (first in, first out) for the inventory valuation	
(d)	Including non-production period costs in the inventory valuation	

7 Aspects of budgeting

7.1 The Accounts Supervisor of Darnbrook Limited provides you with the following information:

- at 20,000 units of output, total costs are £350,000
- at 30,000 units of output, total costs are £500,000

You are to use the high/low method to identify the amount of fixed costs. The supervisor tells you that there is a constant unit variable cost up to this volume, and that there are no stepped fixed costs.

Fill in the following with your answer:

Fixed costs, at these levels of output are   £ ⎡   ⎤

7.2   Croome Limited makes controllers for hot water systems – both domestic and commercial use. The company has prepared a budget for the next quarter for one of its controllers, CC8. This controller is produced in batches and the budget is based on selling and producing 1,000 batches.

One of the customers of Croome Limited has indicated that it may be significantly increasing its order level for controller CC8 for the next quarter and it appears that activity levels of 1,500 batches and 1,800 batches are feasible.

The semi-variable costs should be calculated using the high/low method. If 3,000 batches are sold the total semi-variable cost will be £8,000 and there is a constant unit variable cost up to this volume.

Complete the table below and calculate the budgeted profit per batch of CC8 at the different activity levels.

Batches produced and sold	1,000	1,500	1,800
	£	£	£
Sales revenue	45,000		
Variable costs:			
• Direct materials	10,000		
• Direct labour	12,000		
• Overheads	8,000		
Semi-variable costs:	4,000		
• Variable element			
• Fixed element			
Total cost	34,000		
Total profit	11,000		
Profit per batch (to 2 decimal places)	11.00		

7.3   The budget for direct materials is £6,300; the actual cost is £6,100. The budget for direct labour is £8,900; the actual cost is £9,250.

Which **one** of the following statements is correct?

(a)	Direct materials variance £200 adverse; direct labour variance £350 adverse	
(b)	Direct materials variance £200 favourable; direct labour variance £350 favourable	
(c)	Direct materials variance £200 adverse; direct labour variance £350 favourable	
(d)	Direct materials variance £200 favourable; direct labour variance £350 adverse	

7.4   A budget for 10,000 units of output shows a direct materials cost of £5,600 and a direct labour cost of £8,200. Actual output is 11,000 units.

Which **one** of the following gives the correct figures for the flexed budget?

(a)	Direct materials £5,600; direct labour £8,200	
(b)	Direct materials £5,600; direct labour £9,020	
(c)	Direct materials £6,160; direct labour £9,020	
(d)	Direct materials £6,160; direct labour £8,200	

7.5 Identify the correct variance from the causes of variances given by putting a tick in the relevant column of the table below.

Cause of variance		Adverse	Favourable
(a)	Decrease in material prices		
(b)	More materials are wasted		
(c)	More expensive direct materials are used		
(d)	Specifications are changed to use cheaper materials		
(e)	A lower paid grade of direct labour is employed		
(f)	More efficient use of direct labour		
(g)	During the recession direct labour agrees to work an extra hour a week for no pay		
(h)	The cost of power for the machines increases		
(i)	Selling prices are reduced		
(j)	A decrease in the number of units sold		

7.6 You work as an accounts assistant for Chorlton Limited, a manufacturing business.

You have been given the original budget costs and the actual performance for last month for product CH05. Actual output was 95 per cent of budgeted output.

You are to complete the table below to show a flexed budget and the resulting variances against the budget. Show the actual variance amount for each cost in the column headed 'Variance'.

Note:

• Adverse variances must be denoted with a minus sign or brackets.

• Enter 0 where any figure is zero.

	Original budget	Flexed budget	Actual	Variance
Output level	100%	95%	95%	
	£	£	£	£
Direct materials	3,600		3,500	
Direct labour	9,400		9,350	
Fixed overheads	7,500		7,300	
TOTAL	20,500		20,150	

7.7   Melia Ltd has budgeted to manufacture and sell 50,000 units of product M55 for the year ending 31 December. Howovor, due to a shortage of raw materials, it was only able to manufacture and sell 45,000 units.

(1)   Complete the following table to show a flexed budget and the resulting variances against this budget for the year. Show the actual variance amount, for sales revenue and each cost, in the column headed 'Variance'.

Note:

- Adverse variances must be denoted with a minus sign or brackets.
- Enter 0 where any figure is zero.

	Original budget	Flexed budget	Actual	Variance
Units sold	50,000	45,000	45,000	
	£000	£000	£000	£000
Sales revenue	1,200		1,050	
Less costs:				
Direct materials and direct labour	300		260	
Variable overheads	400		410	
Fixed overheads	350		330	
Profit from operations	150		50	

(2)   Which **one** of the following might have caused the variance for variable overheads?

(a)	A reduction in the price of variable overheads	
(b)	An increase in the price of variable overheads	
(c)	Switching to a cheaper supplier of variable overheads	
(d)	More efficient use of variable overheads	

7.8   Rehman Ltd budgeted to manufacture and sell 6,000 units of product R10 for the year ending 31 December. However, due to an increase in demand it was able to manufacture and sell 6,450 units.

(1)   Complete the following table to show a flexed budget and the resulting variances against this budget for the year. Show the actual variance amount, for sales revenue and each cost, in the column headed 'Variance'.

Note:

- Adverse variances must be denoted with a minus sign or brackets.

- Enter 0 where any figure is zero.

	Original budget	Flexed budget	Actual	Variance
Units sold	6,000	6,450	6,450	
	£000	£000	£000	£000
Sales revenue	840		910	
Less costs:				
Direct materials	160		190	
Direct labour	240		255	
Fixed overheads	280		300	
Profit from operations	160		165	

(2)   Referring to your answer for part (1), which **one** of the variances has had the greatest impact in decreasing profit from operations?

(a)	Sales revenue	
(b)	Direct materials	
(c)	Direct labour	
(d)	Fixed overheads	

7.9 Scimitar Limited, a manufacturing business, has prepared budgeted information for three of its products, SC21, SC29 and SC46 for the next financial year.

Product	SC21	SC29	SC46
Sales revenue (£)	30,600	47,900	52,300
Direct materials (£)	12,250	16,200	26,850
Direct labour (£)	10,860	18,750	19,350

The company expects to produce and sell 10,000 units of SC21 and 15,000 units of SC29. The budgeted sales demand for SC46 is 10% greater than that of SC29. Budgeted fixed overheads are £31,040.

Complete the table below (to two decimal places) to show the budgeted contribution per unit of SC21, SC29 and SC46 sold, and the company's budgeted profit or loss for the year from these products.

	SC21 £	SC29 £	SC46 £	Total £
Selling price per unit				
Less: variable costs per unit				
Direct materials				
Direct labour				
Contribution per unit				
Sales volume (units)				
Total contribution				
Less: fixed overheads				31,040
Budgeted *profit/loss				

*delete as appropriate

8 Short-term decisions

8.1 Bert Peters is the owner of a petrol filling station. He provides you with the following information:

cost of petrol from oil company	£1.20 per litre
selling price	£1.25 per litre
fixed costs for the week	£750

(a) As an accounts assistant, you are to complete the following table showing his weekly costs, sales revenue and profit or loss:

Units of output (litres)	Fixed costs £	Variable costs £	Total cost £	Sales revenue £	Profit/(loss) £
0					
5,000					
10,000					
15,000					
16,000					
17,000					
18,000					
19,000					
20,000					

(b) If sales are currently 18,000 litres each week, calculate the margin of safety, expressed in litres, as a percentage (to the nearest percentage point).

Margin of safety at sales of 18,000 litres	litres	%

8.2   Angrave Limited makes a product which is numbered AN02. The selling price of product AN02 is £22 per unit and the total variable cost is £14 per unit. Angrave Limited estimates that the fixed costs per quarter associated with this product are £12,000.

(a)   Calculate the breakeven volume, in units per quarter, for product AN02.

	units

(b)   Calculate the breakeven sales revenue, in £ per quarter, for product AN02.

£

(c)   Complete the table below to show the budgeted margin of safety in units, and the margin of safety percentage if Angrave Limited sells 2,000 units or 2,500 units of product AN02 per quarter.

Units of AN02 sold per quarter	2,000	2,500
Margin of safety (units)		
Margin of safety (percentage)		

(d)   If Angrave Limited wishes to make a profit of £6,000 per quarter, how many units of AN02 must it sell?

	units

(e)   If Angrave Limited increases the selling price of AN02 by £1, what will be the impact on the breakeven point and the margin of safety per quarter, assuming no change in the number of units sold?

(a)	The breakeven point will decrease and the margin of safety will increase	
(b)	The breakeven point will stay the same but the margin of safety will decrease	
(c)	The breakeven point will decrease and the margin of safety will stay the same	
(d)	The breakeven point will increase and the margin of safety will decrease	

8.3   Nikko Limited has made the following estimates for next month:

Selling price	£20 per unit
Variable cost	£15 per unit
Fixed costs for the month	£100,000
Forecast output	25,000 units
Maximum output	35,000 units

As an accounts assistant, you are to carry out the following tasks:

Task 1

Calculate:

The profit-volume (PV) ratio	
The breakeven point in units next month	
The breakeven point in sales revenue next month	
The margin of safety in units at the forecast output for next month	
The number of units to generate a profit of £50,000 next month	

Task 2

Calculate the profit at:

The forecast output for next month	
The maximum output for next month	

8.4 Wyvern Porcelain Limited produces decorated porcelain figures which are sold in quality shops both in the UK and abroad.

There are three ranges of porcelain figures – 'people', 'animals' and 'birds'. The expected monthly costs and sales information for each range is as follows:

Product	'People'	'Animals'	'Birds'
Sales and production units*	1,000	2,000	2,700
Labour hours per month	1,500	1,000	900
Total sales revenue	£60,000	£55,000	£47,250
Total direct materials	£5,000	£6,000	£5,400
Total direct labour	£15,000	£10,000	£9,000
Total variable overheads	£10,000	£9,000	£8,000

*note: a unit is a porcelain figure

The total expected monthly fixed costs relating to the production of all porcelain figures are £45,400.

As an accounts assistant at Wyvern Porcelain Limited, you are to carry out the following tasks.

Task 1

Complete the table below to show for each product range the expected contribution per unit (to the nearest penny).

Product	'People' £	'Animals' £	'Birds' £
Selling price per unit			
Less: Unit variable costs			
Direct materials			
Direct labour			
Variable overheads			
Contribution per unit			

Task 2

If the company only produces the 'People' range, calculate the number of units it would need to make and sell each month to cover the fixed costs of £45,400.

Breakeven point for the 'People' range	units

Task 3

Making and painting the porcelain figures are highly skilled tasks, and unskilled labour cannot be brought in to cover for absent staff.

Because of staff holidays, the available labour hours for next month are reduced from 3,400 to 2,800. The finance director asks you to calculate the contribution of each unit (porcelain figure) per labour hour.

Using the data from Task 1, complete the table below (rounded to two decimal places).

Note that while the answer should be to two decimal places, when multiplying you should use as many decimal places as your calculator will allow to provide the most accurate answer.

Product	'People'	'Animals'	'Birds'
Contribution per unit			
Labour hours per unit			
Contribution per labour hour			

Task 4

Using the data from Task 3, calculate how many units of each of product ranges 'People', 'Animals' and 'Birds' the company should make and sell in order to maximise its profits using 2,800 labour hours. Complete the table below to show the company's production plan for next month.

'People'	units
'Animals'	units
'Birds'	units

8.5 The Last Company is famous for its 'Snowdon' range of hill-walking boots. The management of the company is considering the production for next year and has asked for help with certain financial decisions.

The following information is available:

wholesale selling price (per pair)	£60
direct materials (per pair)	£20
direct labour (per pair)	£18
production overheads (fixed)	£200,000 per year

The company is planning to manufacture 12,500 pairs of boots next year.

You are to calculate:

- the absorption cost per pair

- the marginal cost per pair

- the profit or loss if 12,500 pairs of boots are sold

A mail order company, Sales-by-Post Limited, has approached The Last Company with a view to selling the 'Snowdon' boot through its catalogue. Sales-by-Post offers two contracts:

- either 2,500 pairs of boots at £45 per pair

- or 5,000 pairs of boots at £37 per pair

As The Last Company usually sells through specialist shops, it is not expected that 'normal' sales will be affected. These 'special orders' are within the capacity of the factory and production overheads will remain unchanged.

As an accounts assistant, you are to advise the management whether these offers should be accepted; illustrate your answer with statements of profit or loss.

8.6 Which **one** of these ethical considerations applies to reporting decisions to employers and clients?

(a)	Professional knowledge and skill is maintained in order to provide a competent service to employers and clients	
(b)	A subjective approach should be used in the preparation of reports for employers and clients	
(c)	The office trainee can prepare reports and present them to employers and clients	
(d)	The presentation of reports to employers and clients should be practised beforehand with a group of friends	

9 Long-term decisions

TABLE OF DISCOUNTED CASH FLOW FACTORS (to three decimal places)								
Cost of capital/ rate of return	10%	12%	14%	16%	18%	20%	22%	24%
Year 1	0.909	0.893	0.877	0.862	0.847	0.833	0.820	0.806
Year 2	0.826	0.797	0.769	0.743	0.718	0.694	0.672	0.650
Year 3	0.751	0.712	0.675	0.641	0.609	0.579	0.551	0.524
Year 4	0.683	0.636	0.592	0.552	0.516	0.482	0.451	0.423
Year 5	0.621	0.567	0.519	0.476	0.437	0.402	0.370	0.341
Year 6	0.564	0.507	0.456	0.410	0.370	0.335	0.303	0.275

Tutorial note: In Assessments you will always be given the appropriate factors.

9.1 The following information relates to two major capital investment projects being considered by Newell Limited. For financial reasons, only one project can be accepted.

	Project Ess	Project Tee
	£	£
Initial cost at the beginning of the project	−100,000	−115,000
Net cash inflows, year: 1	40,000	50,000
2	60,000	35,000
3	20,000	30,000
4	20,000	30,000
5	10,000	30,000
Expected scrap value at end of year 5	5,000	7,500

The initial cost occurs at the beginning of the project and you may assume that the net cash inflows will arise at the end of each year. Newell Limited requires an annual rate of return of 10 per cent, and a maximum payback period of two-and-a-half years.

To help the Managing Director of Newell Limited make her decision, as accounts assistant **you are to:**

- Produce numerical assessments of the two projects based on the following capital investment appraisal methods:

  (a)   the payback period

  (b)   the net present value

- Complete the comparison table (below) and indicate whether or not each project meets the company's investment criteria.
- Advise, in a sentence, which capital investment, if either, should be undertaken, and why.

Appraisal method	Notes	Company policy	Project Ess	Project Tee
Payback period		2.5 years maximum		
Net present value (NPV)	Discount at 10% cost of capital	Accept if positive		
Advice to Newell Limited:				

9.2 A capital investment project has the following expected cash flows over its life of three years:

	£
Initial cost at the beginning of the project	−55,000
Net cash inflows, year: 1	19,376
2	28,491
3	21,053

The expected scrap value at the end of year 3 is nil.

You are to:

(a) Calculate the net present value of the project at annual rates of return of 10 per cent, 12 per cent and 14 per cent. Calculate all money amounts to the nearest £.

(b) What do your calculations in part (a) tell you about this project?

9.3 You work as an accounts assistant for Chester Carpet Limited, which makes quality carpets. Currently you are working on the appraisal of a capital investment project to purchase a new machine for the production department in December 20-1.

The machine will cost £65,000 and will have a useful life of four years. The cash inflows are expected to be:

	£
20-2	17,000
20-3	25,000
20-4	31,000
20-5	24,000

At the end of the project, the machine will be sold as scrap for an expected amount of £4,000.

Chester Carpet Limited requires an annual rate of return of 10 per cent for net present value, and a maximum payback period of three years.

Task 1

Use the working paper on the next page to calculate the payback period and the net present value of the proposed project. Ignore inflation and calculate all money amounts to the nearest £.

Task 2

Write a report, dated 24 November 20-1, to the General Manager evaluating the proposal from a financial viewpoint. State any assumptions you have made in your analysis.

CHESTER CARPET LIMITED

Working paper for the financial appraisal of a new machine for the production department

PAYBACK PERIOD

Year	Cash Flow	Cumulative Cash Flow
	£	£
20-1	_____	_____
20-2	_____	_____
20-3	_____	_____
20-4	_____	_____
20-5	_____	_____

Payback period = _____ (round up to the next month)

DISCOUNTED CASH FLOW

Year	Cash Flow	Discount Factor at 10%	Discounted Cash Flow
	£		£
20-1	_____	1.000	_____
20-2	_____	0.909	_____
20-3	_____	0.826	_____
20-4	_____	0.751	_____
20-5	_____	0.683	_____
Net Present Value (NPV)			_____

9.4   A business is considering a capital investment project. The accounts assistant has prepared the following net present value calculations for the project:

Cost of Capital	Net Present Value
10%	£4,720
12%	£3,040
14%	£1,420
16%	(£80)
18%	(£1,520)

(a)   What is the internal rate of return for this project (to the nearest two percentage points)?

(b)   The business can borrow money for the project from its bank at a rate of 10%. Advise the business whether or not it should go ahead with this project on the basis of the financial information available to you.

9.5   The directors of Chen Ltd ask you to calculate the internal rate of return for a project they are planning to undertake.

The following information is available to you:

- at a cost of capital of 10%, the project gives a positive net present value of £5,510

- at a cost of capital of 20%, the project gives a negative net present value (ie net present cost) of £8,570

You are to use interpolation to calculate the internal rate of return of the project (to the nearest whole percentage).

9.6 Towan Kitchens Limited makes 'flat-pack' kitchens which are sold to the public in DIY stores. You are an accounts assistant and have just received the following email from the General Manager.

EMAIL

From: General Manager

To: Accounts Assistant

Subject: Manufacture of kitchen worktops

Date: 15 September 20-4

As you know, the manufacture of worktops is currently contracted out to another company at a cost to us of £200,000 per year. The production manager has proposed that we should buy the special equipment needed to do the work ourselves in-house, thus making savings on the costs of the contract work. The equipment will cost £300,000 and we will also have to pay the following costs over the next five years:

	operators' wages £	repairs and maintenance £	other costs £
20-5	42,000	8,000	33,000
20-6	64,000	12,000	37,000
20-7	68,000	22,000	42,000
20-8	68,000	25,000	44,000
20-9	70,000	30,000	45,000

If we go ahead, the equipment will be bought at the end of this year ready for production to start in 20-5. At the end of 20-9 the equipment will have a scrap value of £10,000.

Please appraise this proposal from a financial viewpoint. I need to know the payback period and the net present value. As you know, the maximum required payback period is three years and, for net present value, we require a return of 14%.

Task 1

Use the working paper on the next page to calculate the payback period and the net present value of the proposed investment. Ignore inflation and calculate all money amounts to the nearest £.

Task 2

Write a report, dated 18 September 20-4, to the General Manager evaluating the proposal from a financial viewpoint. State any assumptions you have made in your analysis.

TOWAN KITCHENS LIMITED

Working paper for the financial appraisal of in house worktop manufacture

CASH FLOWS

Year	Savings £	Total Costs £	Cash Flow £
20-4	–		
20-5			
20-6			
20-7			
20-8			
20-9			

PAYBACK PERIOD

Year	Cash Flow £	Cumulative Cash Flow £
20-4		
20-5		
20-6		
20-7		
20-8		
20-9		

Payback period = _____ (round up to the next month)

DISCOUNTED CASH FLOW

Year	Cash Flow £	Discount Factor at 14%	Discounted Cash Flow £
20-4		1.000	
20-5		0.877	
20-6		0.769	
20-7		0.675	
20-8		0.592	
20-9		0.519	
Net Present Value (NPV)			

9.7   Bridge Limited is an engineering company. It needs to replace an automated machine that is nearing the end of its working life

Estimates have been made for the initial capital cost, sales income and operating costs of the replacement machine, which is expected to have a useful life of three years, at the end of which it will be sold for £15,000.

	Year 0 £000	Year 1 £000	Year 2 £000	Year 3 £000
Capital expenditure	−75			
Disposal				15
Other cash flows:				
Sales revenue		65	80	55
Operating costs		−30	−35	−35

The company appraises capital investment projects using a 10% cost of capital.

(a)   Complete the table below and calculate the net present value of the proposed replacement machine (to the nearest £000).

	Year 0 £000	Year 1 £000	Year 2 £000	Year 3 £000
Capital expenditure				
Disposal				
Sales revenue				
Operating costs				
Net cash flows				
PV factors	1.0000	0.9091	0.8264	0.7513
Discounted cash flows				
Net present value				

Tick to show if the net present value is:

	positive	
or	negative	

(b)   Calculate the payback period of the proposed replacement machine in years and months. Partial months must be rounded up to the next month.

The payback period is [＿＿＿＿＿＿] year(s) and [＿＿＿＿＿＿] months.

9.8   Farrow Ltd is considering a possible capital investment project.

It will base its decision upon using three appraisal methods, the results of which are shown below:

Appraisal method	Notes	Company policy	Project results
Payback period		3 years	3.5 years
Net present Value (NPV)	Discount at 12% cost of capital	Accept if positive	−£4,000
Internal Rate of Return (IRR)	Discount at 12% cost of capital	Must exceed cost of capital	−5.5%

The company considers Net Present Value to be the most important investment criteria.

Identify the correct recommendation for each decision in the table below.

Select your entries for the 'Recommendation' column from the following list:

Accept as positive

Reject as more than 3 years

Reject as negative

Accept as more than 3 years

Reject as per most important investment criteria

Accept as greater than the cost of capital

Reject as lower than the cost of capital

Accept as per most important investment criteria

Appraisal method	Recommendation
Payback period	
NPV	
IRR	
Overall	

Answers to chapter activities

An Introduction to cost accounting

1.1

Statement	Financial accounting	Cost accounting
Reports relate to what has happened in the past	✔	
May be required by law	✔	
Gives estimates of costs and income for the future		✔
May be made public	✔	
Gives up-to-date reports which can be used for controlling the business		✔
Is used by people outside the business	✔	
Is designed to meet the requirements of people inside the business		✔
Shows details of the expected costs of materials, labour and expenses		✔
Records accurate amounts, not estimates	✔	

1.2   (a)   Rent of premises

1.3   (c)   Raw materials to make the product

1.4

REPORT

To: The Partners
From: Accounts Assistant
Date: today

Costs and revenue for last year

I report on the details of the costs and revenue for last year of each office of the practice. Details are as follows:

	Triangle	South Toynton	St Faiths
Cost Centre	*£000*	*£000*	*£000*
• materials	75	70	80
• labour	550	650	730
• expenses	82	69	89
• total	707	789	899
Profit Centre			
Revenue	950	869	1,195
less Costs (see above)	707	789	899
Profit	243	80	296
Investment Centre			
Profit (see above)	243	80	296
Investment	750	900	1,150
Expressed as a percentage	32%	9%	26%
Revenue Centre	950	869	1,195

1.5

		Fixed	Semi-variable	Variable
(a)	Rent of business premises	✔		
(b)	Week's hire of machinery at £100 per week for one particular job	✔		
(c)	Telephone system with a fixed line rental and a cost per call		✔	
(d)	Supervisor's wages	✔		
(e)	Diminishing (reducing) balance depreciation	✔		
(f)	Production-line employees paid a basic wage, with a bonus linked to output		✔	
(g)	Royalty paid to author for each book sold			✔
(h)	Accountant's fees	✔		
(i)	Raw materials used in production			✔

1.6

Cost item	Classification (write your answer)
Insurance of buildings	indirect expense
Salaries of office staff	indirect labour
Zip fasteners	direct materials
Electricity	indirect expense*
Wages of factory supervisors	indirect labour
Pay of machine operators	direct labour
Consignment of blue denim cloth	direct materials
Stationery for the office	indirect materials
Television advertising	indirect expense
Oil for production machines	indirect materials
Fuel for delivery vans	indirect materials
Wages of canteen staff	indirect labour

*The cost of electricity has been classified above as an indirect expense. This is often the case because it is not worthwhile analysing the cost of power for each unit of production. Where machines are used that take a lot of power, meters are often fitted to each machine so that costs may be identified and allocated to production as a direct expense. Whichever treatment – indirect expense or direct expense – it is important that it is applied consistently.

1.7

Cost item	Total cost	Prime cost	Production overhead costs	Admin- istration costs	Selling and distribution
	£	£	£	£	£
Wages of employees working on pre-fabrication line	19,205	19,205			
Supervisors' salaries	5,603		5,603		
Materials for making pre-fabricated panels	10,847	10,847			
Cleaning materials for factory machinery	315		315		
Sundry factory expenses	872		872		
Salaries of office staff	6,545			6,545	
Repairs to sales staff cars	731				731
Depreciation of office equipment	200			200	
Magazine advertising	1,508				1,508
Sundry office expenses	403			403	
Hire of display stands used at garden centres	500				500
Office stationery	276			276	
TOTALS	47,005	30,052	6,790	7,424	2,739

1.8 (d) Accounting staff are straightforward and honest in all professional and business relationships

2 Materials costs

2.1 (c) 100 boxes

2.2 (b) Inventory is valued in accordance with IAS2, *Inventories*

2.3

DATE 20-3	DESCRIPTION	FIFO £	AVCO £
21 June	Total issue value*	6,350	6,450
30 June	Total closing inventory value**	1,175	1,075

Workings:

*FIFO:	2,000 units issued at £2.00 per unit	=	£4,000
	1,000 units issued at £2.35 per unit	=	£2,350
			£6,350

AVCO:	(£4,000 + £3,525) ÷ 3,500 units	=	£2.15 per unit
	3,000 units issued at £2.15 per unit	=	£6,450

**FIFO:	500 units at £2.35 per unit	=	£1,175
AVCO:	500 units at £2.15 per unit	=	£1,075

2.4

INVENTORY RECORD: FIFO

Product: Material Wye

Date	Receipts			Issues			Balance		
20-1	Quantity (kg)	Cost per kg £	Total Cost £	Quantity (kg)	Cost per kg £	Total Cost £	Quantity (kg)	Cost per kg £	Total Cost £
1 Aug	Balance						5,000	5.00	25,000
10 Aug	2,000	5.25	10,500				5,000	5.00	25,000
							2,000	5.25	10,500
							7,000		35,500
18 Aug	3,000	5.50	16,500				5,000	5.00	25,000
							2,000	5.25	10,500
							3,000	5.50	16,500
							10,000		52,000
23 Aug				5,000	5.00	25,000			
				2,000	5.25	10,500			
				1,000	5.50	5,500	2,000	5.50	11,000
				8,000		41,000			

INVENTORY RECORD: AVCO

Product: Material Zed

Date	Receipts			Issues			Balance		
20-1	Quantity (kg)	Cost per kg £	Total Cost £	Quantity (kg)	Cost per kg £	Total Cost £	Quantity (kg)	Cost per kg £	Total Cost £
1 Aug	Balance						10,000	4.00	40,000
6 Aug	5,000	4.30	21,500				10,000	4.00	40,000
							5,000	4.30	21,500
							15,000	4.10	61,500
19 Aug	6,000	4.45	26,700				15,000	4.10	61,500
							6,000	4.45	26,700
							21,000	4.20	88,200
24 Aug				12,000	4.20	50,400	9,000	4.20	37,800

Tutorial note:

To assist you, full workings have been shown, however, AAT Assessment tasks often state that only one entry is permitted per inventory cell.

2.5 **(a)**

INVENTORY RECORD: FIFO

Product: Photocopying paper (reams)

Date	Receipts			Issues			Balance		
20-8	Quantity (reams)	Cost per ream £	Total Cost £	Quantity (reams)	Cost per ream £	Total Cost £	Quantity (reams)	Cost per ream £	Total Cost £
1 Feb	Balance						100	2.00	200
5 Feb				50	2.00	100	50	2.00	100
10 Feb	150	2.20	330				50	2.00	100
							150	2.20	330
							200		430
15 Feb				50	2.00	100			
				50	2.20	110	100	2.20	220
				100		210			
18 Feb	200	2.30	460				100	2.20	220
							200	2.30	460
							300		680
24 Feb				100	2.20	220			
				20	2.30	46	180	2.30	414
				120		266			

(b)

INVENTORY RECORD: AVCO									
Product: Photocopying paper (reams)									

Date	Receipts			Issues			Balance		
20-8	Quantity (reams)	Cost per ream £	Total Cost £	Quantity (reams)	Cost per ream £	Total Cost £	Quantity (reams)	Cost per ream £	Total Cost £
1 Feb	Balance						100	2.00	200
5 Feb				50	2.00	100	50	2.00	100
10 Feb	150	2.20	330				50	2.00	100
							150	2.20	330
							200	2.15	430
15 Feb				100	2.15	215	100	2.15	215
18 Feb	200	2.30	460				100	2.15	215
							200	2.30	460
							300	2.25	675
24 Feb				120	2.25	270	180	2.25	405

Tutorial note:

To assist you, full workings have been shown, however, AAT Assessment tasks often state that only one entry is permitted per inventory cell.

2.6   Task 1

INVENTORY RECORD: FIFO Product: White plastic								
Date	Receipts			Issues			Balance	
	Quantity (kg)	Cost per kg £	Total Cost £	Quantity (kg)	Cost per kg £	Total Cost £	Quantity (kg)	Total Cost £
20-9								
Balance at 1 April							20,000	20,000
7 April	10,000	1.10	11,000				30,000	31,000
12 April				25,000	1.02	25,500	5,000	5,500
20 April	20,000	1.20	24,000				25,000	29,500
23 April				15,000	1.167	17,500	10,000	12,000

Workings:

7 April: 20,000 kg at £1.00 + 10,000 kg at £1.10, total 30,000 kg = £31,000
12 April: 20,000 kg at £1.00 + 5,000 kg at £1.10, total 25,000 kg = £25,500
20 April: 5,000 kg at £1.10 = £5,500 + 20,000 kg at £1.20 = £24,000, total 25,000 kg = £29,500
23 April: 5,000 kg at £1.10 + 10,000 kg at £1.20, total 15,000 kg = £17,500

Task 2

20-9	Code number	Debit £	Credit £
7 April	2000	11,000	
7 April	3000		11,000
12 April	2100	25,500*	
12 April	2000		25,500
20 April	2000	24,000	
20 April	3000		24,000
23 April	2100	17,500**	
23 April	2000		17,500

*£20,000 + £5,500
**£5,500 + £12,000

2.7   **(a)**

$$\text{Economic Order Quantity (EOQ)} = \sqrt{\frac{2 \times 36,125 \text{ kg} \times £30}{£3}}$$

$$= \sqrt{\frac{2,167,500}{£3}}$$

$$= \sqrt{722,500}$$

$$= \underline{850 \text{ kg}}$$

(b) and **(c)**

Inventory record for metal grade X8

Date	Receipts			Issues			Balance	
	Quantity (kg)	Cost per kg £	Total Cost £	Quantity (kg)	Cost per kg £	Total Cost £	Quantity (kg)	Total Cost £
Balance as at 22 May							420	1,512
24 May	850	3.711	3,154				1,270	4,666
26 May				900	3.674	3,307	370	1,359
27 May	850	3.755	3,192				1,220	4,551
30 May				800	3.730	2,984	420	1,567

2.8

	Cost
FIFO issue	£97,800
AVCO issue	£99,120
FIFO balance	£46,750
AVCO balance	£45,430

2.9

Statement	FIFO	LIFO	AVCO
Issues from inventory are from the most recent receipts		✔	
In times of rising prices, reported profits will usually be lower than with other methods		✔	
Closing inventory is based on more recent costs of goods received	✔		
Issues from inventory are from the earliest receipts	✔		
Acceptable for tax purposes	✔		✔
Closing inventory is valued at a weighted average cost			✔
Permitted by IAS 2, *Inventories*	✔		✔
In times of rising prices, the cost of sales figure will usually be lower than with other methods	✔		
Closing inventory is based on older costs of goods received		✔	

3 Labour costs

3.1

Employee	Basic pay £	Overtime rate 1 £	Overtime rate 2 £	Gross pay for week £
L Constantinou	448.00	–	96.00	544.00
H Gunther	525.00	40.00	22.50	587.50
J White	357.00	68.00	30.60	455.60

3.2

Employee	Time rate £	Piecework rate £	Gross pay for week £
J Daniels	456.00	440.00	456.00
L Ho	402.50	422.50	422.50
T Turner	423.00	450.00	450.00

3.3

Employee	Time rate £	Bonus £	Gross pay for week £
H Hands	437.50	25.00	462.50
A Khan	434.75	0.00	434.75
T Shah	418.00	11.00	429.00
D Smith	512.00	9.60	521.60

3.4   **Task 1**

Dr		**Wages control account**		Cr
	£			£
Cash/bank (net wages)	8,000	Production (direct labour)		7,750
HM Revenue & Customs (income tax and NIC)	1,650	Production overheads (indirect labour)		1,500
Pension contributions	850	Non-production overheads (administration)		1,250
	10,500			10,500

Task 2

20-9	Code number	Debit £	Credit £
18 June	2100	7,750	
18 June	3100		7,750
18 June	2200	1,500	
18 June	3100		1,500
18 June	2300	1,250	
18 June	3100		1,250

3.5   **(a)**

> **Total cost of direct labour for February:**
>
> | | | | | £ |
> | --- | --- | --- | --- | --- |
> | 2,600 hours | x | £10 per hour | = | 26,000 |
> | 400 hours | x | £15 (£10 + £5) per hour | = | 6,000 |
> | 3,000 | | | | 32,000 |

(b)

Account name	Account code	Debit £	Account name	Account code	Credit £
Production – 'Porth boards'	2100	32,000	Wages control	4400	32,000

3.6

Employee:	S Patton		Profit Centre: Moulding			
Employee number: 617			Basic pay per hour: £12.00			
	Hours spent on production	**Hours worked on indirect work**	**Notes**	**Basic pay £**	**Overtime premium £**	**Total pay £**
Monday	6	0		72	0	72
Tuesday	7	0		84	6	90
Wednesday	6	2	10am-12noon training	96	12	108
Thursday	8	0		96	12	108
Friday	6	1	8am-9am maintenance	84	6	90
Saturday	4	0		48	12	60
Sunday	2	0		24	24	48
Total	39	3		504	72	576

3.7 **(a)** £574, ie 41 standard hours at £14

(b) £592, ie Monday £100, Tuesday £112, Wednesday £126, Thursday £154, Friday £100

(c) £574, ie standard hours produced is above the minimum guaranteed

(d) £610, ie 40 actual hours at £14, plus bonus £50

3.8 **(a)**

Labour cost	Hours	£
Basic pay	320	3,840
Overtime rate 1	25	375
Overtime rate 2	25	450
Total cost before team bonus	370	4,665
Bonus payment		600
Total cost including team bonus		5,265

(b) The direct labour cost per equivalent unit for April is **£0.81**

(c) The equivalent units of production with regard to labour for May will be **6,350** and the bonus payable will be **£434**

3.9

Statement	Time rate	Piecework rate	Bonus system
The gross pay calculation is: hours worked x rate per hour	✔		
Method used for repetitive work where output is more important than quality		✔	
The gross pay calculation is: gross pay + proportion of the time saved			✔
The employer has to set time allowances for work done		✔	✔
Pay is not linked to output	✔		
Employees can earn more by working harder		✔	✔
There is no pressure on time, so quality of output should be maintained	✔		
The amount earned by employees varies with output		✔	✔
The gross pay calculation is: number of items produced x rate per item		✔	

4 Overheads and expenses

4.1

OVERHEAD ANALYSIS		
January 20-7		
	Accountancy Department	**Management Department**
Budgeted total overheads (£)	15,884	19,855
Budgeted teaching hours	722	1,045
Budgeted overhead absorption rate (£)	22	19

OVERHEAD ANALYSIS		
Course: Finance for Managers		
	Accountancy Department	**Management Department**
Teaching hours	45	20
Budgeted overhead absorption rate (£)	22	19
Overhead absorbed by course (£)	990	380

4.2

WYEVALE PROCESSING LIMITED
BUDGETED PRODUCTION OVERHEAD SCHEDULE
for next month

Budgeted overheads	Basis of apportionment	Totals £	Processing £	Packing £	Quality Assurance £	Stores £	Maintenance £
Rent and rates	Floor area	4,500	1,200	1,575	375	600	750
Supervisors' salaries	Number of employees	3,690	1,230	1,722	246	246	246
Depreciation of equipment	Equipment usage	2,640	1,800	600	240	–	–
Canteen costs	Number of employees	720	240	336	48	48	48
TOTAL		11,550	4,470	4,233	909	894	1,044

4.3

Budgeted overheads	Day care ward £	Surgical ward £	Operating theatre £	Administration £	Totals £
Overheads	28,750	42,110	32,260	9,075	112,195
Reapportion Administration	1,650	4,125	3,300	−9,075	
Reapportion Operating theatre	20,320	15,240	−35,560		
Total overheads to patient wards	50,720	61,475			112,195

The fixed element of the telephone and internet costs that will be apportioned to the day care ward is **£1,767**

The variable element of the telephone and internet costs that will be apportioned to the surgical ward is **£1,862**

4.4 Task 1

Budgeted overheads for four weeks ended 28 April 20-2	Basis of apportion-ment	Totals £	New Car Sales £	Used Car Sales £	Servicing £	Administration £
Depreciation of non-current assets	Carrying amount	8,400	2,100	1,260	4,200	840
Rent of premises	Floor space	10,000	4,000	3,000	2,000	1,000
Other property overheads	Floor space	4,500	1,800	1,350	900	450
Staff costs	Allocated	35,295	11,080	7,390	9,975	6,850
Administration overheads	Allocated	3,860				3,860
		62,055	18,980	13,000	17,075	13,000
Administration			2,600	3,900	6,500	-13,000
		62,055	21,580	16,900	23,575	

Task 2
Budgeted overhead absorption rate for the servicing centre:
£23,575 ÷ 1,025 hours =

£23.00 per direct labour hour

4.5

Budgeted overheads	Basis of apportionment	Cutting £	Assembly £	Maintenance £	Stores £	Admin £	Totals £
Depreciation charge for machinery	Carrying amount of machinery	3,000	1,200				4,200
Power for production	Power usage	1,800	240				2,040
Rent and rates of premises	Floor space	6,600	4,400	1,100	1,760	2,640	16,500
Light and heat for premises	Floor space	5,100	3,400	850	1,360	2,040	12,750
Indirect labour	Allocated			38,550	29,850	51,250	119,650
Totals		16,500	9,240	40,500	32,970	55,930	155,140
Reapportion Maintenance		30,375	10,125	−40,500			
Reapportion Stores		19,782	13,188		−32,970		
Reapportion Administration		27,965	27,965			−55,930	
Total overheads to profit centres		94,622	60,518				155,140

4.6 **(1)** (c) Moulding £9 per hour; finishing £22 per hour

(2) (d) Moulding £16 per hour; finishing £15 per hour

(3) (d) Moulding under-absorbed £1,600; finishing over-absorbed £900

4.7 **(1)** (c) 40 per cent

    (2) (b) £27,500

4.8

Dr		Production overheads account: Kitchen Department (2100)		Cr
	£			£
Bank (overheads incurred)	5,000	Production		5,600
Statement of profit or loss (over-absorption)	600			
	5,600			5,600

Dr		Production overheads account: Canning Department (2200)		Cr
	£			£
Bank (overheads incurred)	3,500	Production		3,200
		Statement of profit or loss (under-absorption)		300
	3,500			3,500

20-6	Code number	Debit £	Credit £
16 June	2000	£5,600	
16 June	2100		£5,600
16 June	2000	£3,200	
16 June	2200		£3,200
16 June	2100	£600	
16 June	4000		£600
16 June	4000	£300	
16 June	2200		£300

5   Methods of costing

5.1   Task 1

<table>
<tr><td colspan="4" align="center">JOB NO 12345
Poetry book for John Dun</td></tr>
<tr><td></td><td colspan="3" align="center">NUMBER OF COPIES</td></tr>
<tr><td></td><td align="center">500</td><td align="center">1,000</td><td align="center">2,000</td></tr>
<tr><td></td><td align="center">£</td><td align="center">£</td><td align="center">£</td></tr>
<tr><td>Fixed Costs</td><td></td><td></td><td></td></tr>
<tr><td>Setting up machine</td><td>60.00</td><td>60.00</td><td>60.00</td></tr>
<tr><td>Artwork</td><td>84.00</td><td>84.00</td><td>84.00</td></tr>
<tr><td>Page setting</td><td>300.00</td><td>300.00</td><td>300.00</td></tr>
<tr><td>Direct Materials</td><td></td><td></td><td></td></tr>
<tr><td>Paper</td><td>200.00</td><td>400.00</td><td>800.00</td></tr>
<tr><td>Other printing consumables</td><td>100.00</td><td>200.00</td><td>400.00</td></tr>
<tr><td>Direct Labour</td><td>65.00</td><td>130.00</td><td>260.00</td></tr>
<tr><td>Production Overheads
(80% of direct labour costs)</td><td>52.00</td><td>104.00</td><td>208.00</td></tr>
<tr><td>TOTAL COST</td><td>861.00</td><td>1,278.00</td><td>2,112.00</td></tr>
<tr><td>Profit (25% of total cost)</td><td>215.25</td><td>319.50</td><td>528.00</td></tr>
<tr><td>SELLING PRICE</td><td>1,076.25</td><td>1,597.50</td><td>2,640.00</td></tr>
</table>

Task 2

	Cost per book to author:
500 copies	£2.15
1,000 copies	£1.60
2,000 copies	£1.32

5.2 **(a)** £1.37 (£12,450 + £8,100) ÷ 15,000 units

(b) £1.11 (£30,000 − £4,700) ÷ 15,000 units

(c) £1.80 (£12,450 + £8,100 + £6,450) ÷ 15,000 units

(d) £27,000 £12,450 + £8,100 + £6,450

(e) £31,800 £36,000 − £4,200

(f) (d) Period costs

5.3

Cost element	Costs	Completed units	Work-in-progress			Total equivalent units	Cost per unit	WIP valuation
			Units	% complete	Equivalent units			
	A	B	C	D	E	F	G	H
					C x D	B + E	A ÷ F	E x G
	£						£	£
Direct materials	10,725	2,750	500	100	500	3,250	3.30	1,650
Direct labour	6,600	2,750	500	50	250	3,000	2.20	550
Production overheads	3,900	2,750	500	50	250	3,000	1.30	325
Total	21,225						6.80	2,525

5.4   **(a)**   **Note:** normal loss, with scrap sales

Dr				Process Account			Cr
	Quantity (litres)	Unit cost	Total cost		Quantity (litres)	Unit cost	Total cost
		£	£			£	£
Materials	65,000	0.30	19,500	Normal loss	5,000	0.05	250
Labour		0.20	13,000	Finished goods	60,000	0.70	42,000
Overheads		0.15	9,750				
	65,000		42,250		65,000		42,250

Tutorial note:

The cost per unit of the expected output is:

$$\frac{£42,250 - £250}{60,000 \text{ litres}} = £0.70 \text{ per litre}$$

(b)

	Debit £	Credit £
Normal loss	250	

5.5   **Note:** abnormal gain

Dr				Process Account				Cr
	Quantity (kilos)	Unit cost	Total cost		Quantity (kilos)	Unit cost	Total cost	
		£	£			£	£	
Materials	84,000	0.20	16,800	Normal loss	4,000	0.20	800	
Labour		0.15	12,600	Finished goods	81,000	0.41	33,210	
Overheads		0.05	4,200					
			33,600					
Abnormal gain	1,000	0.41	410					
	85,000		34,010		85,000		34,010	

Tutorial note:

The cost per unit of the expected output is:

$$\frac{£33,600 - £800}{80,000 \text{ kilos}} = £0.41 \text{ per kilo}$$

Dr	Normal Loss Account		Cr
	£		£
Process account	800	Bank/trade receivables	600
		Abnormal gain account	*200
	800		800

Dr	Abnormal gain account		Cr
	£		£
Normal loss account	*200	Process account	410

*1,000 kilos at 20p per kilo

5.6   **Note:** normal loss with scrap sales

Dr				Process 1 Account			Cr
	Quantity (kilos)	Unit cost	Total cost		Quantity (kilos)	Unit cost	Total cost
		£	£			£	£
Materials	5,000	0.40	2,000	Normal loss (5%)	250	0.20	50
Labour		0.20	1,000	Transfer to			
Overheads		0.10	500	process 2	4,500	0.73	3,268
							3,318
				Abnormal loss	250	0.73	182
	5,000		3,500		5,000		3,500

Note: abnormal gain

Dr				Process 2 Account			Cr
	Quantity (kilos)	Unit cost	Total cost		Quantity (kilos)	Unit cost	Total cost
		£	£			£	£
Transfer from				Normal loss (3%)	135	0.40	54
process 1	4,500	0.73	3,268	Finished goods	4,400	1.15	5,054
Labour		0.25	1,125				
Overheads		0.15	675				
			5,068				
Abnormal gain	35	1.15	40				
	4,535		5,108		4,535		5,108

Tutorial notes:

*   In process 1, the cost per unit of the expected output is:

$$\frac{£3,500 - £50}{4,750 \text{ kilos}} = £0.73 \text{ per kilo (to the nearest penny, but note that £0.7263 is used to calculate total cost)}$$

*   In process 2, the cost per unit of the expected output is:

$$\frac{£5,068 - £54}{4,365 \text{ kilos}} = £1.15 \text{ per kilo (to the nearest penny, but note that £1.1487 is used to calculate total cost)}$$

5.7 **(a)**

Description	Kilos	Unit cost £	Total cost £	Description	Kilos	Unit cost £	Total cost £
Material ZC6	300	1.60	480	Normal loss	100	0.50	50
Material ZC8	1,500	0.80	1,200	Output	1,900	7.50	14,250
Material ZC10	200	1.50	300				
Labour			6,720				
Overheads			5,600				
	2,000		14,300		2,000		14,300

Tutorial Note:

The cost per unit of the expected output is:

$$\frac{£14,300 - £50}{1,900 \text{ kilos}} = £7.50 \text{ per kilo}$$

(b)

	Debit	Credit
Process	✔	
Abnormal gain		✔

6 Marginal, absorption and activity based costing

6.1

Marginal cost per seat	£55.00
Absorption cost per seat	£80.00
Profit or loss if 4,000 seats are sold	£30,000.00

Workings:

Marginal cost per seat	£
Direct materials	25.00
Direct labour	30.00
MARGINAL COST	55.00

Absorption cost per seat	£
Direct materials	25.00
Direct labour	30.00
Fixed production overheads £100,000 ÷ 4,000 seats	25.00
ABSORPTION COST	80.00

OUTDOOR LIMITED
Statement of profit or loss: 4,000 seats

	£	£
Sales revenue (4,000 x £100)		400,000
Direct materials (4,000 x £25)	100,000	
Direct labour (4,000 x £30)	120,000	
Fixed production overheads	100,000	
TOTAL COST		320,000
GROSS PROFIT		80,000
Less non-production overheads		50,000
NET PROFIT		30,000

6.2 **(a)**

STRELLIS LIMITED

Statement of profit or loss for the month ended 30 June 20-5

	Marginal costing		Absorption costing	
	£	£	£	£
Sales revenue 3,500 units at £10 each		35,000		35,000
Variable costs				
Direct materials at £2.50 each	10,000		10,000	
Direct labour at £3.00 each	12,000		12,000	
Prime cost	22,000		22,000	
Less Closing inventory (marginal cost*)				
500 units at £5.50 each	2,750			
	19,250			
Fixed production overheads	15,000		15,000	
			37,000	
Less Closing inventory (absorption cost*)				
500 units at £9.25 each			4,625	
Less Cost of sales		34,250		32,375
Gross profit		750		2,625
Less non-production overheads		1,500		1,500
Net profit/(loss)		(750)		1,125

*Closing inventory is calculated on the basis of this year's costs:

marginal costing, variable costs only, ie £2.50 + £3.00 = £5.50 per unit x 500 units = £2,750

absorption costing, variable and fixed costs,
ie £37,000 ÷ 4,000 units = £9.25 per unit x 500 units = £4,625

(b) The difference in the profit and loss figures is caused only by the closing inventory figures: £2,750 under marginal costing, and £4,625 under absorption costing.

With marginal costing, the full amount of the fixed production overheads has been charged in this year's statement of profit or loss; by contrast, under absorption costing, part of the fixed production overheads (here £15,000 x 12.5%* = £1,875) has been carried forward in the inventory valuation.

*500 units of closing inventory out of 4,000 units manufactured

6.3   **(a)**   Activity based costing is a costing method which charges overheads to production on the basis of activities. The cost per unit of a product can be calculated based on its use of activities.

The steps to applying activity based costing are:

- The cost driver – the factor which influences the costs – is identified, and the rate for each cost is calculated, eg the cost of placing a purchase order for goods to be used in production.

- The rate for each cost is charged to production, based on the use of the activity, eg if a product requires two purchase orders to be placed, it will be charged with the cost of two activities.

(b)   •   In capital-intensive industries, overheads often form a high proportion of total costs and are complex in nature. They need to be accounted for in a more sophisticated way than would be the case under absorption costing, eg absorbing overhead costs under one basis – such as direct labour hours – does not acknowledge the complex nature of the overheads and production processes.

•   Often modern flexible manufacturing methods require short production runs, with the ability to switch from one product to another at short notice. This is in contrast to older industries where the same product is produced over a long production run. These differing production methods impact on costs such as setting up equipment, which will be much larger per unit of production for small production runs than for large ones. Activity based costing is able to charge the cost of overheads to production on the basis of activities – something which absorption costing would not do.

6.4   **(a)**   *calculation of weekly overheads for set ups and quality inspections*

			£	£
set ups:	product Cee	5 x £250	1,250	
	product Dee	50 x £250	12,500	
				13,750
quality inspection:	product Cee	5 x £150	750	
	product Dee	50 x £150	7,500	
				8,250
TOTAL				22,000

At present the weekly overheads are charged on the basis of labour hours:

	£
product Cee (500 hours)	11,000
product Dee (500 hours)	11,000
TOTAL	22,000

(b)   *activity based costing:*

	£	£
product Cee		
5 set ups at £250	1,250	
5 quality inspections £150	750	
		2,000
product Dee		
50 set ups at £250	12,500	
50 quality inspections £150	7,500	
		20,000
TOTAL		22,000

(c)   • By using activity based costing, there is a more accurate reflection of the cost of the activities of set up and quality inspection.

• The cost of 50,000 units of product Cee is reduced by £9,000 (ie £11,000 – £2,000), while the cost of 50,000 units of product Dee is increased by £9,000 (ie from £11,000 to £20,000).

• This may well have implications for the viability of product Dee, and for the selling prices of both products.

6.5   (d)   Including non-production period costs in the inventory valuation

(Does not comply with the requirements of IAS 2, *Inventories*, and the ethical principle of professional competence.)

7   Aspects of budgeting

7.1   •

		30,000 units	£500,000
high output	30,000 units	£500,000
less low output	20,000 units	£350,000
equals difference	10,000 units	£150,000

•   amount of variable cost per unit:

$$\frac{£150,000}{10,000} = £15 \text{ variable cost per unit}$$

•   at 20,000 units of output the cost structure is:

total cost	£350,000
less variable costs (20,000 units x £15 per unit)	£300,000
equals fixed costs	£ 50,000

•   check at 30,000 units of output when the cost structure is:

variable costs (30,000 units x £15 per unit)	£450,000
add fixed costs (as above)	£ 50,000
equals total costs	£500,000

Fixed costs, at these levels of output are **£50,000**

7.2

Batches produced and sold	1,000	1,500	1,800
	£	£	£
Sales revenue	45,000	67,500	81,000
Variable costs:			
• Direct materials	10,000	15,000	18,000
• Direct labour	12,000	18,000	21,600
• Overheads	8,000	12,000	14,400
Semi-variable costs:	4,000		
• Variable element		3,000	3,600
• Fixed element		2,000	2,000
Total cost	34,000	50,000	59,600
Total profit	11,000	17,500	21,400
Profit per batch (to 2 decimal places)	11.00	11.67	11.89

7.3 (d) Direct materials variance £200 favourable; direct labour variance £350 adverse

7.4 (c) Direct materials £6,160; direct labour £9,020

7.5 (a), (d), (e), (f) and (g) are favourable; (b), (c), (h), (i) and (j) are adverse

7.6

	Original budget	Flexed budget	Actual	Variance
Output level	100%	95%	95%	
	£	£	£	£
Direct materials	3,600	3,420	3,500	−80
Direct labour	9,400	8,930	9,350	−420
Fixed overheads	7,500	7,500	7,300	200
TOTAL	20,500	19,850	20,150	−300

7.7   **(1)**

	Original budget	Flexed budget	Actual	Variance
Units sold	50,000	45,000	45,000	
	£000	£000	£000	£000
Sales revenue	1,200	1,080	1,050	−30
Less costs:				
Direct materials and direct labour	300	270	260	10
Variable overheads	400	360	410	−50
Fixed overheads	350	350	330	20
Profit from operations	150	100	50	−50

(2)   (b)   An increase in the price of variable overheads

7.8   **(1)**

	Original budget	Flexed budget	Actual	Variance
Units sold	6,000	6,450	6,450	
	£000	£000	£000	£000
Sales revenue	840	903	910	7
Less costs:				
Direct materials	160	172	190	−18
Direct labour	240	258	255	3
Fixed overheads	280	280	300	−20
Profit from operations	160	193	165	−28

(2)   **(d)**   Fixed overheads

7.9

	SC21 £	SC29 £	SC46 £	Total £
Selling price per unit	3.06	3.19	3.17	
Less: variable costs per unit				
Direct materials	1.23	1.08	1.63	
Direct labour	1.09	1.25	1.17	
Contribution per unit	0.74	0.86	0.37	
Sales volume (units)	10,000	15,000	16,500	
Total contribution	7,400	12,900	6,105	26,405
Less: fixed overheads				31,040
Budgeted ~~profit~~/loss				4,635

Tutorial note: if total amounts (rather than per unit amounts to two decimal places) are used, the contribution amounts are SC21 £7,490, SC29 £12,950, SC46 £6,100. These give a total contribution of £26,540, which results in a budgeted loss of £4,500.

8 Short-term decisions

8.1   **(a)**

Units of output (litres)	Fixed costs £	Variable costs £	Total cost £	Sales revenue £	Profit/(loss) £
0	750	0	750	0	(750)
5,000	750	6,000	6,750	6,250	(500)
10,000	750	12,000	12,750	12,500	(250)
15,000	750	18,000	18,750	18,750	0
16,000	750	19,200	19,950	20,000	50
17,000	750	20,400	21,150	21,250	100
18,000	750	21,600	22,350	22,500	150
19,000	750	22,800	23,550	23,750	200
20,000	750	24,000	24,750	25,000	250

(b)

Margin of safety at sales of 18,000 litres	3,000 litres	17%

Tutorial note:

current output – breakeven output = 18,000 litres – 15,000 litres = 3,000 litres

$$\frac{\text{current output} - \text{breakeven output}}{\text{current output}} \times \frac{100}{1}$$

$$= \frac{18,000 \text{ litres} - 15,000 \text{ litres}}{18,000 \text{ litres}} = 16.67\% = 17\%$$

8.2   **(a)**   **1,500** units

$$\frac{\text{Fixed costs}}{\text{Contribution per unit}} = \frac{£12,000}{£8^*}$$

*£22 – £14

(b)   **£33,000**

1,500 units x £22

(c)

Units of AN02 sold per quarter	2,000	2,500
Margin of safety (units)	500	1,000
Margin of safety (percentage)	25	40

(d)   **2,250** units

$$\frac{£12,000 + £6,000 \text{ (target profit)}}{£8}$$

(e)   (a)   The breakeven point will decrease and the margin of safety will increase

8.3 **Task 1**

The profit-volume (pv) ratio	0.25 or 25%
The breakeven point in units next month	20,000 units
The breakeven point in sales revenue next month	£400,000
The margin of safety in units at the forecast output for next month	5,000 units
The number of units to generate a profit of £50,000 for next month	30,000 units

Workings:

- profit-volume (PV) ratio

$$\frac{\text{contribution (£)}}{\text{selling price (£)}} = \frac{£5^*}{£20} = 0.25 \text{ or } 25\%$$

  * selling price £20 – variable cost £15

- breakeven point in units next month

$$\frac{\text{fixed costs (£)}}{\text{contribution per unit (£)}} = \frac{£100,000}{£5} = 20,000 \text{ units}$$

- breakeven point in sales revenue next month

$$\frac{\text{fixed costs (£)}}{\text{PV ratio}} = \frac{£100,000}{0.25} = £400,000$$

  check: 20,000 units x selling price £20 per unit = £400,000

- margin of safety at output of 25,000 units next month

$$\frac{\text{current output – breakeven output}}{\text{current output}} = \frac{25,000 - 20,000}{25,000} = 5,000 \text{ units}$$

- number of units to generate a profit of £50,000 next month

$$\frac{\text{fixed costs (£) + target profit (£)}}{\text{contribution per unit (£)}} = \frac{£100,000 + £50,000}{£5} = 30,000 \text{ units}$$

Task 2

The forecast output for next month	£25,000
The maximum output for next month	£75,000

Workings:

		forecast output (25,000 units) £	maximum output (35,000 units) £
	sales revenue (at £20 each)	500,000	700,000
less	variable costs (at £15 each)	375,000	525,000
equals	contribution (to fixed costs and profit)	125,000	175,000
less	monthly fixed costs	100,000	100,000
equals	forecast profit for month	25,000	75,000

8.4   **Task 1**

Product	'People' £	'Animals' £	'Birds' £
Selling price per unit	60	27.50	17.50
Less: Unit variable costs			
Direct materials	5	3.00	2.00
Direct labour	15	5.00	3.33
Variable overheads	10	4.50	2.96
Contribution per unit	30	15.00	9.21

Task 2

Breakeven point for the 'People' range is:

$$\frac{\text{fixed costs (£)}}{\text{contribution per unit (£)}} = \frac{£45,400}{£30} = \underline{1,514 \text{ units}}$$

Task 3 (Please see note on question 8.4 [page 67] for guidance on the use of decimal places)

Product	'People'	'Animals'	'Birds'
Contribution per unit	£30	£15	£9.21
Labour hours per unit	1.5	0.5	0.33*
Contribution per labour hour	£20	£30	£27.63

*three units produced per hour = 0.33 hours

Task 4

- Labour hours are the limiting factor here, with only 2,800 hours available.
- To maximise profits, the company should maximise the contribution from each labour hour.
- The preferred order is 'Animals' (at £30 contribution per labour hour), 'Birds' (at £27.63), and 'People' (at £20).
- The company's production plan will be:

'Animals', 2,000 units x 0.5 hours per unit	=	1,000 hours
'Birds', 2,700 units x 0.33 hours per unit	=	900 hours
'People', 600 units x 1.5 hours per unit	=	900 balance of hours available
		2,800 hours

Note that this production plan does not allow for full production of the 'People' range.

8.5   **Absorption cost**

		£
direct materials (per pair)		20.00
direct labour (per pair)		18.00
production overheads (fixed)	£200,000 ÷ 12,500 pairs	16.00
ABSORPTION COST (per pair)		54.00

Marginal cost

	£
direct materials (per pair)	20.00
direct labour (per pair)	18.00
MARGINAL COST (per pair)	38.00

Profit or loss at existing production of 12,500 pairs of boots, see below.

THE LAST COMPANY
Statements of profit or loss

	Existing production 12,500 pairs of boots £	Existing production + 2,500 pairs @ £45 each £	Existing production + 5,000 pairs @ £37 each £
Sales revenue (per year):			
12,500 pairs at £60 each	750,000	750,000	750,000
2,500 pairs at £45 each	–	112,500	–
5,000 pairs at £37 each	–	–	185,000
	750,000	862,500	935,000
Less production costs:			
Direct materials (£20 per pair)	250,000	300,000	350,000
Direct labour (£18 per pair)	225,000	270,000	315,000
Production overheads (fixed)	200,000	200,000	200,000
PROFIT	75,000	92,500	70,000

The conclusion is that the first special order should be accepted and the second declined.

8.6   (a)   Professional knowledge and skill is maintained in order to provide a competent service to employers and clients

9 Long-term decisions

9.1 (a) payback period

	PROJECT ESS		PROJECT TEE	
Year	Cash Flow	Cumulative Cash Flow	Cash Flow	Cumulative Cash Flow
	£000	*£000*	*£000*	*£000*
0	−100	−100	−115	−115
1	40	−60	50	−65
2	60	−	35	−30
3	20	20	30	−
4	20	40	30	30
5	*15	55	*37.5	67.5
	*includes scrap value			

As can be seen from the above table:

- Project Ess pays back after two years
- Project Tee pays back after three years

(b)   net present value

Year	Discount Factor	PROJECT ESS Cash Flow £000	PROJECT ESS Discounted Cash Flow £000	PROJECT TEE Cash Flow £000	PROJECT TEE Discounted Cash Flow £000
0	1.000	−100	−100	−115	−115
1	0.909	40	36.36	50	45.45
2	0.826	60	49.56	35	28.91
3	0.751	20	15.02	30	22.53
4	0.683	20	13.66	30	20.49
5	0.621	15	9.32	37.5	23.29
Net Present Value (NPV)			23.92		25.67

Appraisal method	Notes	Company policy	Project Ess	Project Tee
Payback period		2.5 years maximum	2 years ✔	3 years ✗
Net present value (NPV)	Discount at 10% cost of capital	Accept if positive	£23,920 ✔	£25,670 ✔

Advice to Newell Limited:
Project Ess is to be preferred as it meets both of the investment criteria

9.2   **(a)**

Year	Cash Flow £		Discount Factor 10%		Discounted Cash Flow £
Year 0	−55,000	x	1.000	=	−55,000
Year 1	19,376	x	0.909	=	17,613
Year 2	28,491	x	0.826	=	23,534
Year 3	21,053	x	0.751	=	15,811
			Net Present Value (NPV)	=	1,958

Year	Cash Flow £		Discount Factor 12%		Discounted Cash Flow £
Year 0	−55,000	x	1.000	=	−55,000
Year 1	19,376	x	0.893	=	17,303
Year 2	28,491	x	0.797	=	22,707
Year 3	21,053	x	0.712	=	14,990
			Net Present Value (NPV)	=	nil

Year	Cash Flow £		Discount Factor 14%		Discounted Cash Flow £
Year 0	−55,000	x	1.000	=	−55,000
Year 1	19,376	x	0.877	=	16,993
Year 2	28,491	x	0.769	=	21,910
Year 3	21,053	x	0.675	=	14,211
			Net Present Value (NPV)	=	(1,886)

(b)

- At an annual rate of return of 10%, the net present value is positive so it is worth going ahead with the project.

- At an annual rate of return of 12%, the net present value is nil, so 12% is the internal rate of return (IRR) of this project, ie the rate of return at which the present value of the cash inflows exactly balances the initial investment, that is 'breaks even'. As there is no positive net present value, the project will be rejected.

- At an annual rate of return of 14%, the net present value is negative, so the project will be rejected.

9.3 Task 1

CHESTER CARPET COMPANY LIMITED

Working paper for the financial appraisal of a new machine for the production department

PAYBACK PERIOD

Year	Cash Flow	Cumulative Cash Flow	
	£	£	
20-1	−65,000	−65,000	
20-2	17,000	−48,000	
20-3	25,000	−23,000	
20-4	31,000	8,000	£23,000* required
20-5	**28,000	36,000	

*£31,000 − £8,000

Payback period = 2 years + (£23,000/£31,000) = 2 years and 9 months (rounded up to the next month)

DISCOUNTED CASH FLOW

Year	Cash Flow	Discount Factor at 10%	Discounted Cash Flow
	£		£
20-1	−65,000	1.000	−65,000
20-2	17,000	0.909	15,453
20-3	25,000	0.826	20,650
20-4	31,000	0.751	23,281
20-5	**28,000	0.683	19,124
Net Present Value (NPV)			13,508

**£24,000 + £4,000 scrap value

Task 2

REPORT
To: General Manager   **From:** Accounts Assistant   **Date:** 24 November 20-1
<u>Purchase of a new machine for the production department</u>   I have carried out an appraisal of the above project. The proposal to purchase the new machine is acceptable from a financial viewpoint for the following reasons: • The payback period is during 20-4. If we assume even cash flows during the year, the payback period can be calculated as 2.7 years (or 2 years and 9 months) from the start. This is acceptable since it is shorter than the company requirement of three years, although there is not a great deal of room for error in the cash flow calculations.   • The project returns a positive net present value of £13,508 at a discount rate of 10%. This calculation assumes that all cash flows occur at the end of each year.

9.4 **(a)** The internal rate of return for this project is approximately 16%, ie the rate at which net present value is closest to nil. This is the rate at which the present value of the project 'breaks even'.

(b) An IRR of approximately 16% is higher than the 10% borrowing cost. This means that, in financial terms, the project is acceptable – the wider the margin of IRR above the cost of capital (here, the borrowing cost), the better.

9.5

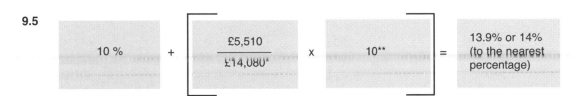

$$10\% \; + \; \left[\; \frac{£5,510}{£14,080^{*}} \; \times \; 10^{**} \; \right] \; = \; \begin{array}{l} 13.9\% \text{ or } 14\% \\ \text{(to the nearest} \\ \text{percentage)} \end{array}$$

*£5,510 + £8,570 = £14,080

**20 – 10 = 10

9.6   Task 1

TOWAN KITCHENS LIMITED

Working paper for the financial appraisal of in-house worktop manufacture

CASH FLOWS

Year	Savings	Total Costs	Cash Flow
	£	£	£
20-4	–	–300,000	–300,000
20-5	200,000	–83,000	117,000
20-6	200,000	–113,000	87,000
20-7	200,000	–132,000	68,000
20-8	200,000	–137,000	63,000
20-9	200,000	*–135,000	65,000

*costs total £145,000 less scrap value £10,000

Tutorial note: for 2005 to 2009 total costs are: operators' wages + repairs and maintenance + other costs

PAYBACK PERIOD

Year	Cash Flow	Cumulative Cash Flow	
	£	£	
20-4	–300,000	–300,000	
20-5	117,000	–183,000	
20-6	87,000	–96,000	
20-7	68,000	–28,000	
20-8	63,000	35,000	£28,000* required
20-9	65,000	100,000	

* £63,000 – £35,000

Payback period = 3 years + (£28,000/£63,000) = 3 years and 6 months (rounded up to the next month)

DISCOUNTED CASH FLOW

Year	Cash Flow	Discount Factor at 14%	Discounted Cash Flow
	£		£
20-4	–300,000	1.000	–300,000
20-5	117,000	0.877	102,609
20-6	87,000	0.769	66,903
20-7	68,000	0.675	45,900
20-8	63,000	0.592	37,296
20-9	65,000	0.519	33,735
Net Present Value (NPV)			–13,557

Task 2

REPORT
To: General Manager
From: Accounts Assistant
Date: 18 September 20-4

Purchase of equipment to manufacture worktops

I have carried out an appraisal of the above project. Unfortunately, the proposal to purchase the new equipment is not acceptable from a financial viewpoint for the following reasons:

- The payback period is during 20-8. If we assume even cash flows during the year, the payback period can be calculated as 3.4 years (or 3 years and 5 months) from the start. This is longer than the company requirement of three years, and so the project is not acceptable.

- The project returns a negative net present value of £13,557 at a discount rate of 14%. This calculation assumes that all cash flows occur at the end of each year. At a lower rate of return, for example 10%, the project would be acceptable with a positive net present value.

9.7   (a)

	Year 0 £000	Year 1 £000	Year 2 £000	Year 3 £000
Capital expenditure	−75			
Disposal				15
Sales revenue		65	80	55
Operating costs		−30	−35	−35
Net cash flows	−75	35	45	35
PV factors	1.0000	0.9091	0.8264	0.7513
Discounted cash flows	−75	32	37	26
Net present value	20			

positive	✔
negative	

(b)   The payback period is 1 year and 11 months (rounded up to the next month)

9.8

Appraisal method	Recommendation
Payback period	Reject as more than 3 years
NPV	Reject as negative
IRR	Reject as lower than the cost of capital
Overall	Reject as per most important investment criteria

Practice assessment 1

This Practice Assessment contains ten tasks and you should attempt to complete every task.
Each task is independent. You will not need to refer to your answers to previous tasks.
Read every task carefully to make sure you understand what is required.

Where the date is relevant, it is given in the task data.
Both minus signs and brackets can be used to indicate negative numbers unless task instructions say otherwise.

You must use a full stop to indicate a decimal point. For example, write 100.57 NOT 100,57 or 100 57
You may use a comma to indicate a number in the thousands, but you don't have to. For example, 10000 and 10,000 are both acceptable.

Task 1

Westlake Ltd uses raw material M5 in the manufacture of its products. The company had the following quantities of M5 in inventory:

Date purchased	Quantity (kg)	Cost per kilo £	Total cost £
4 December	350	2.40	840
9 December	500	2.50	1,250
14 December	400	2.65	1,060

From the following amounts, insert the correct cost into the cost column of the table below to record the issue of 800 kg of M5 on 15 December and to record the inventory balance after the issue using:

• FIFO (first in, first out)

• AVCO (weighted average cost)

Amounts:

£1,090   £1,965

£1,134   £1,970

£1,185   £2,016

£1,560   £2,060

	Cost
FIFO issue	
AVCO issue	
FIFO balance	
AVCO balance	

Task 2

Westlake Limited uses the following accounts to record payroll transactions in its cost bookkeeping system:

- wages control
- production direct costs
- operating overheads
- non-operating overheads

For each of the four transactions in the following table show the account which will be debited, the account which will be credited and the amount of the payment.

Select from the following accounts:

Non-operating overheads, Operating overheads, Production direct costs, Wages control.

Transaction	Account debited	Account credited	Amount £
1 Paid wages of direct labour employees. 270 hours at £14 per hour.			
2 Paid wages of factory supervisors. Basic pay £2,200 + £150 overtime.			
3 Paid wages of stores department staff. £1,050 + 10% bonus.			
4 Paid wages of general administration department staff. £1,760 + 20% bonus.			

Task 3

Westlake Limited has a Production Department where the employees work in teams of two. Their basic rate is £11.00 per hour and there are two rates of overtime as follows:

Overtime rate 1: basic pay + 25%

Overtime rate 2: basic pay + 50%

Westlake sets a target for production of every component each month. A team bonus equal to 10% of basic hourly rate is payable for every unit of production in the month in excess of the target.

The target for June for team 8 was 5,000 units.

In June the production was 5,500 units.

(a) Complete the gaps in the table below to calculate the total labour cost for team 8.

Labour cost	Hours	£
Basic pay	210	
Overtime rate 1	20	
Overtime rate 2	30	
Total cost before team bonus	260	
Bonus payment		
Total cost including team bonus		

(b) Calculate the total labour cost per unit of the finished production for June.

Give your answer in £s to two decimal places.

The total labour cost per unit for June is £ [   ]

There are two employees in team 8.

(c) Complete the following sentence:

The basic pay and overtime for each member of team 8 for June was £ [   ] and the bonus payable to each team member was £ [   ].

Task 4

Westlake Limited has the following information for its two profit centres and three support department cost centres:

Budgeted overheads	£	£
Depreciation charge for machinery		4,450
Power for production		2,970
Rent and rates of premises		8,550
Light and heat for premises		2,250
Indirect labour costs:		
Maintenance	16,400	
Stores	30,300	
Administration	35,650	
Totals	82,350	18,220

Additional information				
Department	Carrying amount of machinery	Production machinery power usage (KwH)	Floor space (square metres)	Number of employees
Profit centres:				
Cutting	30,000	8,000	350	3
Finishing	20,000	2,000	250	2
Support department cost centres:				
Maintenance			70	1
Stores			120	2
Administration			110	3
Total	50,000	10,000	900	11

Overheads are allocated or apportioned on the most appropriate basis. The total overheads of the support departments' cost centres are then reapportioned to the two profit centres, in the following way:

* 50% of the Maintenance cost centre's time is spent maintaining production machinery in the Cutting profit centre, 40% in the Finishing profit centre, and the remainder in the Administration department.

* The Stores cost centre makes 70% of its issues to the Cutting profit centre, and 30% to the Finishing profit centre.

* Administration supports the two profit centres equally.

Use the following table to allocate or apportion the budgeted overheads using the most appropriate basis.

Indicate negative figures with minus signs, NOT brackets.

Select your entries for the 'Basis of apportionment' column from the following list: Allocated, Carrying amount of machinery, Floor space, Number of employees, Production machinery power usage.

Budgeted overheads	Basis of apportionment	Cutting £	Finishing £	Maintenance £	Stores £	Admin £	Totals £
Depreciation charge for machinery							
Power for production							
Rent and rates of premises							
Light and heat for premises							
Indirect labour							
Totals							
Reapportion Maintenance							
Reapportion Stores							
Reapportion Administration							
Total overheads to profit centres							

Task 5

Westlake Limited has prepared budgeted overheads and activity levels for Quarter 1 of next year. The figures for its two production departments are as follows:

Quarter 1 budget	Cutting	Finishing
Budgeted overheads (£)	18,900	10,450
Budgeted direct labour hours	1,350	950
Budgeted machine hours	2,100	1,045

(a) What would be the budgeted overhead absorption rate for each department if this were set based on their both being heavily automated?

Cutting £9 per hour; finishing £10 per hour	
Cutting £9 per hour; finishing £11 per hour	
Cutting £14 per hour; finishing £10 per hour	
Cutting £14 per hour; finishing £11 per hour	

(b) What would be the budgeted overhead absorption rate for each department if this were set based on their both being labour intensive?

Cutting £9 per hour; finishing £10 per hour	
Cutting £9 per hour; finishing £11 per hour	
Cutting £14 per hour; finishing £10 per hour	
Cutting £14 per hour; finishing £11 per hour	

Additional data

At the end of Quarter 1 actual overheads incurred were found to be:

Quarter 1	Cutting	Finishing
Actual overheads (£)	19,300	9,850

(c) Assuming that exactly the same amount of overheads was absorbed as budgeted, what were the budgeted under- or over-absorptions in Quarter 1?

Cutting over-absorbed £400; finishing over-absorbed £600	
Cutting over-absorbed £400; finishing under-absorbed £600	
Cutting under-absorbed £400; finishing under-absorbed £600	
Cutting under-absorbed £400; finishing over-absorbed £600	

Task 6

Westlake Limited, is costing a new product, WL57, which will be produced in batches of 10,000 units.

It has estimated that the following costs will be incurred in producing one batch of 10,000 units of WL57:

Product WL57	£ per batch
Direct materials	6,400
Direct labour	4,300
Variable overheads	2,600
Fixed production overheads	2,700
Administration, selling and distribution costs	1,200
Total costs	17,200

You are to:

(a) Calculate the estimated prime cost of one unit of WL57 (to **two** decimal places).

£ [   ]

(b) Calculate the estimated full absorption cost of one unit of WL57 (to **two** decimal places).

£ [   ]

(c) Calculate the estimated marginal production cost of one unit of WL57 (to **two** decimal places).

£ [   ]

(d) Calculate the estimated prime cost of one batch of WL57.

£ [   ]

(e) Calculate the estimated full absorption cost of one batch of WL57.

£ [   ]

(f)   Which **one** of the following costs will always be included in Westlake's inventory valuation?

(a) Product costs	
(b) Period costs	
(c) Administration costs	
(d) Selling and distribution costs	

(g)   Which **one** of these is an example of ethical behaviour by one of Westlake's accounting technicians?

(a) Calculating profits subjectively	
(b) Treating Westlake's profit as confidential	
(c) Using either marginal or absorption costing in order to maximise profits	
(d) Including the personal costs of Westlake's directors in the business costs	

(h)   Why might Westlake decide to allocate its costs between the products of different departments?

(a) To report the business'/ total profits or losses	
(b) To report segmented assets and liabilities	
(c) To report segmented profits or losses	
(d) To reduce departmental inventory valuations	

(i)   Westlake's Production Department is treated as a profit centre. Which **one** of the following statements is correct?

(a) The Production Department is responsible for its total costs, revenues, assets and liabilities	
(b) The costs of support centres used by the Production Department are apportioned to it	
(c) The inventory of the Production Department is valued at the higher of cost and net realisable value	
(d) Direct labour within the Production Department is paid on a time rate basis so that employees are paid for what they produce	

Task 7

(a)   Choose the correct description for each of the three terms in the table below.

Select your entries for the 'Description' column from the following list:

Selling price plus variable costs
Sales volume where there is neither profit nor loss
Selling price less total costs
Excess of actual sales over breakeven sales
Set amount of profit above breakeven
Profit when selling price equals variable costs
Excess of breakeven sales over actual sales
Sales revenue where there is neither profit nor loss
Planned revenue less costs
Selling price less variable costs

Term	Description
Breakeven units	
Margin of safety	
Target profit	

Westlake Limited makes a product which is coded WL15. The selling price of product WL15 is £24 per unit and the total variable cost is £16 per unit. Westlake Limited estimates that the fixed costs per quarter associated with this product are £1,760.

(b)   Calculate the breakeven volume, in units, for product WL15.

|_____| units

(c)   Calculate the breakeven sales revenue, in £, for product WL15.

£ |_____|

(d)   Complete the table below to show the margin of safety in units, and the margin of safety percentage if Westlake Limited sells 400 units or 500 units of product WL15.

Units of WL15 sold	400	500
Margin of safety (units)		
Margin of safety (percentage)		

(e)   If Westlake Limited wishes to make a target profit of £2,400, how many units of WL15 must it sell?

|_____| units

Task 8

The following eight options describe the behaviour of different types of costs during a short period of one quarter of a year.

Option	Description
1	Increases in total as volume increases
2	Decreases in total as volume increases
3	Increases per unit as selling price increases
4	Decreases per unit as selling price increases
5	Decreases per unit as volume increases
6	Made up of fixed and variable costs
7	Fixed for a certain volume range only
8	Variable for a certain volume range only

Write the option number which shows the correct description for the following four types of cost in the box below.

Cost	Description
Fixed cost	
Variable cost	
Semi-variable cost	
Stepped cost	

Task 9

Westlake Limited budgeted to manufacture 3,000 units of product WL18 last month. However, due to an increase in demand it was able to manufacture and sell 3,240 units.

(1)   Complete the table below to show a flexed budget and the resulting variances against this budget for the month. Show the actual variance amount, for sales revenue and each cost, in the column headed 'Variance'.

Note:

·   Adverse variances must be denoted with a minus sign or brackets.

·   Enter 0 where any figure is zero.

	Original budget	Flexed budget	Actual	Variance
Units sold	3,000	3,240	3,240	
	£	£	£	£
Sales revenue	19,500		22,100	
Less costs:				
Direct materials	5,500		5,800	
Direct labour	4,300		4,900	
Fixed overheads	6,700		7,100	
Profit from operations	3,000		4,300	

(2)   Referring to your answer for part (1), which **one** of the variances has had the greatest impact in increasing profit from operations?

(a)	Sales revenue	
(b)	Direct materials	
(c)	Direct labour	
(d)	Fixed overheads	

(3)   Which **one** of the following might have caused the variance for direct labour?

(a)	More efficient usage of direct labour	
(b)	A decrease in employees' pay	
(c)	A lower paid grade of labour used	
(d)	An increase in employees' pay	

Task 10

One of the machines in the Cutting department is nearing the end of its working life and Westlake Limited is considering purchasing a replacement machine.

Estimates have been made for the initial capital cost, sales income and operating costs of the replacement machine, which is expected to have a working life of three years, at the end of which it will be sold for £6,000:

	Year 0 £000	Year 1 £000	Year 2 £000	Year 3 £000
Capital expenditure	−40			
Disposal				6
Other cash flows:				
Sales revenue		33	40	35
Operating costs		−12	−15	−14

The company appraises capital investment projects using a 10% cost of capital.

(a) Complete the table below and calculate the net present value of the proposed replacement machine (to the nearest £000). Use a minus sign to indicate a negative figure. Enter 0 where any figure is zero.

	Year 0 £000	Year 1 £000	Year 2 £000	Year 3 £000
Capital expenditure				
Disposal				
Sales revenue				
Operating costs				
Net cash flows				
PV factors	1.0000	0.9091	0.8264	0.7513
Discounted cash flows				
Net present value				

Tick to show if the net present value is

	positive	
or	negative	

(b) Calculate the payback period of the proposed replacement machine in years and months. Partial months must be rounded up to the next month.

The payback period is [   ] year(s) and [   ] months.

Practice assessment 2

This Practice Assessment contains ten tasks and you should attempt to complete every task. Each task is independent. You will not need to refer to your answers to previous tasks.
Read every task carefully to make sure you understand what is required.

Where the date is relevant, it is given in the task data.
Both minus signs and brackets can be used to indicate negative numbers unless task instructions say otherwise.

You must use a full stop to indicate a decimal point. For example, write 100.57 NOT 100,57 or 100 57
You may use a comma to indicate a number in the thousands, but you don't have to. For example, 10000 and 10,000 are both acceptable.

Task 1

Clark Ltd has the following information for plastic grade CL5:

- Annual demand – 1,125 kilograms (kg)
- Annual holding cost per kilogram – £10
- Fixed ordering cost – £25

(a) Calculate the Economic Order Quantity (EOQ) for CL5.

EOQ =	kg

The inventory record shown below for plastic grade CL5 for the month of December has only been fully completed for the first three weeks of the month.

(b) Complete the entries in the inventory record for the two receipts on 24 and 29 December that were ordered using the EOQ method.

(c) Complete ALL entries in the inventory record for the two issues in the month and for the closing balance at the end of December using the FIFO method of issuing inventory.

Show the costs per kilogram (kg) in £ to three decimal places, and the total costs in whole £. Only **one** entry is permitted per inventory cell.

Inventory record for plastic grade CL5

Date	Receipts			Issues			Balance	
	Quantity (kg)	Cost per kg £	Total Cost £	Quantity (kg)	Cost per kg £	Total Cost £	Quantity (kg)	Total Cost £
Balance as at 22 December							40	170
24 December		4.40						
28 December				85				
29 December		4.60						
30 December				55				

Task 2

Below are extracts from Clark Ltd's payroll for last week.

Date	Labour costs
7 December	Plastic cutting: Production employees' pay 420 hours at £12 per hour
8 December	Plastic assembly: Production employees' basic pay £4,200 + £300 overtime
10 December	Stores department: Employees' pay £1,600 + 10% bonus
11 December	General Administration department: Staff salaries £2,200 + 15% bonus

Complete the cost journal entries to record the four payroll payments made last week.

Select your entries for the 'Code' column from the following list:

5501	Plastic cutting direct costs
5502	Plastic assembly direct costs
6000	Operating overheads
7000	Non-operating overheads
9000	Wages control account

Date	Code	Dr £	Cr £
7 December			
7 December			
8 December			
8 December			
10 December			
10 December			
11 December			
11 December			

Task 3

Clark Ltd's Maintenance Department incurred the following times last month for servicing machinery.

	Hours
Normal time hours worked	140
Overtime hours worked (paid at time-and-a-half)	12
Overtime hours worked (paid at double time)	15
Total hours worked	167

The maintenance staff's normal time hourly rate is £14 per hour.

Overtime premiums paid are included as part of the maintenance labour cost.

Calculate the following **four** costs for the Maintenance Department and insert the entries into the table below:

(a)   The labour cost of normal time working.

(b)   The overtime premium of time-and-a-half working.

(c)   The total cost of double-time working.

(d)   The total labour cost.

	Cost £
Calculation **(a)**	
Calculation **(b)**	
Calculation **(c)**	
Calculation **(d)**	

Task 4

Clark Ltd calculates depreciation on a reducing balance basis, and allocates/apportions other overheads using the most appropriate basis for each.

(a) Complete the table below to identify a suitable basis for allocating or apportioning each overhead by selecting the most appropriate option.

Select your entries for the 'Basis of apportionment' column from the following list:

Age of cutting equipment

Replacement cost of cutting equipment

Carrying amount of cutting equipment

Number of maintenance employees

Number of quality control inspections

Carrying amount of assembly equipment

Time spent servicing assembly equipment

Administration office floor space

Factory floor space

Overhead	Basis of apportionment
Depreciation of cutting equipment	
Rent and rates of production departments	
Quality control costs	
Assembly equipment maintenance costs	
Assembly equipment insurance costs	

(b) Clark Ltd has already allocated and apportioned its current overhead costs for the next quarter, as shown in the table below. These costs have yet to be reapportioned to the two profit centres of Cutting and Assembly.

The Administration department services the two profit centres, the Maintenance department and the Stores department. These costs are to be reapportioned 40% to the Cutting profit centre; 40% to the Assembly profit centre; and 10% each to the Maintenance and Stores departments.

The Stores costs are reapportioned on the basis of inventory requisitions. The Cutting profit centre expects to have 1,440 requisitions and the Assembly profit centre expects to have 960 requisitions.

The Maintenance department reapportions costs on the basis of maintenance hours. The Cutting profit centre expects to use 1,288 maintenance hours and the Assembly profit centre expects to use 322 maintenance hours.

Complete the table by reapportioning costs on the basis of the information given above. Enter your answers in whole pounds only. Indicate negative figures with minus signs, NOT brackets.

Budgeted overheads	Cutting £	Assembly £	Maintenance £	Stores £	Admin £	Totals £
Depreciation of equipment	3,500	2,500	800	200	500	7,500
Power for production	1,920	1,280				3,200
Rent and rates of premises	3,520	2,640	1,320	440	880	8,800
Light and heat for premises	1,520	1,140	570	190	380	3,800
Indirect labour costs	12,000	16,000	26,200	38,360	49,140	141,700
Administration costs					2,650	2,650
Totals	22,460	23,560	28,890	39,190	53,550	167,650
Reapportion Administration						
Reapportion Stores						
Reapportion Maintenance						
Total overheads to profit centres						

(c) Another overhead is machine running costs. The estimated cost for the next quarter is £54,000, which consists of a fixed element and a variable element. The fixed element is 55% of the total cost and the rest is variable. The fixed element of the total cost is to be apportioned between the Cutting profit centre and the Assembly profit centre in the ratio 68:32. The variable element of the total cost is apportioned in the ratio of 74:26.

Complete the following sentences by inserting the correct values.

The fixed element of the machine running costs that will be apportioned to the Cutting profit centre is.

£ [   ]

The variable element of the machine running costs that will be apportioned to the Assembly profit centre is:

£ [   ]

Task 5

Clark Ltd has the following information for its Cutting and Assembly departments:

Quarter 1	Cutting	Assembly
Budgeted direct labour hours	1,680	520
Budgeted machine hours	1,040	260
Actual direct labour hours	1,730	510
Actual machine hours	1,025	310
Budgeted overheads	£24,700	£8,580
Actual overheads	£26,500	£7,940

(a) The budgeted overhead absorption rate (to two decimal places) for the Cutting department based upon machine hours, and for the Assembly department based upon labour hours, is:

	Cutting £	Assembly £
Budgeted overhead absorption rate	per hour	per hour

(b) Complete the following sentence by selecting the appropriate item and inserting the correct amount:

In Quarter 1 overheads for the Assembly department were

OVER-ABSORBED / UNDER-ABSORBED

by £ [   ]

(c) In Quarter 2, the overhead absorption rate for the Cutting department was £25 per machine hour, the actual overheads incurred were £27,230 and the actual machine hours used were 1,080. Complete the following table:

	Overheads incurred £	Overheads absorbed £	Difference absorbed £	Under/over absorption
Cutting department				

Task 6

Clark Ltd is costing a new product, CL45, which will be produced in batches of 6,000 units.

It has estimated that the following costs will be incurred in producing one batch of 6,000 units of CL45:

Product CL45	£ per batch
Direct materials	6,240
Direct labour	4,320
Variable overheads	1,360
Fixed production overheads	2,960
Administration, selling and distribution costs	1,050
Total costs	15,930

You are to:

(a) Calculate the estimated prime cost of one unit of CL45 (to **two** decimal places).

£ ☐

(b) Calculate the estimated full absorption cost of one unit of CL45 (to **two** decimal places).

£ ☐

(c) Calculate the estimated marginal production cost of one unit of CL45 (to **two** decimal places).

£ ☐

(d) Calculate the estimated prime cost of one batch of CL45.

£ ☐

(e) Calculate the estimated full absorption cost of one batch of CL45.

£ ☐

(f)   Which **one** of the following costs would NEVER be included in Clark's inventory valuation?

(a) Product costs	
(b) Period costs	
(c) Marginal costs	
(d) Prime costs	

(g)   Which of these is an example of unethical behaviour by one of Clark's accounting technicians:

(a) Allocating Clark's costs between products on an objective basis	
(b) Keeping up-to-date with technical and professional developments in accounting	
(c) Using Twitter to disclose Clark's profits to friends	
(d) Using data from the accounting records to calculate revenues in an objective way	

(h)   Why might Clark decide to allocate its costs between the products of different departments?

(a) To comply with accounting standards	
(b) To report segmented assets and liabilities	
(c) To report segmented profits or losses	
(d) To increase overall inventory valuation	

(i)   Clark's Production Department is treated as a profit centre. Which **one** of the following statements is correct?

(a) The Production Department is responsible for its total costs and revenues	
(b) The costs of support centres used by the Production Department are charged to the Administration Department	
(c) The Production Department is responsible for its assets and liabilities	
(d) Supervisory labour costs within the Production Department are treated as a direct cost	

Task 7

(a) Choose the correct description for each of the three terms in the table below.

Select your entries for the 'Description' column from the following list:
- Selling price plus variable costs
- Sales volume where there is neither profit nor loss
- Selling price less total costs
- Excess of actual sales over breakeven sales
- Planned revenue less costs
- Profit when selling price equals variable costs
- Excess of breakeven sales over actual sales
- Sales revenue where there is neither profit nor loss
- Scarce resource which restricts output
- Selling price less variable costs

Term	Description
Contribution	
Limiting factor	
Breakeven revenue	

Clark Ltd makes a product which is coded CL18. The selling price of product CL18 is £15 per unit and the total variable cost is £10 per unit. Clark Ltd estimates that the fixed costs per quarter associated with this product are £2,000.

(b) Calculate the breakeven volume, in units, for product CL18.

> [   ] units

(c) Calculate the breakeven sales revenue, in £, for product CL18.

> £ [   ]

(d) Complete the table below to show the margin of safety in units, and the margin of safety percentage if Clark Ltd sells 500 units or 800 units of product CL18.

Units of CL18 sold	500	800
Margin of safety (units)		
Margin of safety (percentage)		

(e) If Clark Ltd wishes to make a target profit of £750, how many units of CL18 must it sell?

> [   ] units

Task 8

The Cutting department of Clark Ltd uses process costing for some of its products.

The process account for December for one particular process needs to be completed from the following information:

- Inputs of materials were:

  – material CL54   140 kg at £3.50 per kg

  – material CL75   40 kg at £5.00 per kg

  – material CL96   60 kg at £4.50 per kg

- One employee worked on this process during December. The employee worked 34 hours per week for 4 weeks and was paid £11.00 per hour.

- Overheads are absorbed on the basis of £4 per labour hour.

- Clark Ltd expects a normal loss of 5% during this process, which it then sells for £3.00 per kg.

- There is expected to be no abnormal gain or loss.

(a)   Complete the process account below for December.

Process Account							
Description	**kg**	**Unit cost £**	**Total cost £**	**Description**	**kg**	**Unit cost £**	**Total cost £**
Material CL54				Normal loss			
Material CL75				Output			
Material CL96							
Labour							
Overheads							

(b)   Identify the correct entry for each of the following in a process account.

	Debit	**Credit**
Abnormal gain		
Transfer to next process		

Task 9

Clark Ltd has budgeted to manufacture 2,500 units of product CL32 last month. However, due to a shortage of raw materials it was only able to manufacture and sell 2,250 units.

(1) Complete the table below to show a flexed budget and the resulting variances against this budget for the month. Show the actual variance amount, for sales revenue and each cost, in the column headed 'Variance'.

Note:

- Adverse variances must be denoted with a minus sign or brackets.

- Enter 0 where any figure is zero.

	Original budget	Flexed budget	Actual	Variance
Units sold	2,500	2,250	2,250	
	£	£	£	£
Sales revenue	30,200		27,310	
Less costs:				
Direct materials and direct labour	10,600		9,440	
Variable overheads	6,900		6,460	
Fixed overheads	5,400		5,620	
Profit from operations	7,300		5,790	

(2) Referring to your answer for part (1), which **one** of the variances has had the greatest impact in decreasing profit from operations?

(a) Sales revenue	
(b) Direct materials and direct labour	
(c) Variable overheads	
(d) Fixed overheads	

(3)   Which **one** of the following might have caused the variance for sales revenue?

(a) Fewer units have been sold	
(b) A decrease in the selling price	
(c) An increase in the selling price	
(d) Fewer units have been sold and a decrease in the selling price	

Task 10

One of the machines in the Cutting department is nearing the end of its working life and Clark Ltd is considering purchasing a replacement machine.

Estimates have been made for the initial capital cost, sales income and operating costs of the replacement machine, which is expected to have a working life of three years, at the end of which it will be sold for £8,000:

	Year 0 £000	Year 1 £000	Year 2 £000	Year 3 £000
Capital expenditure	−40			
Disposal				8
Other cash flows:				
Sales revenue		25	30	34
Operating costs		−10	−12	−15

The company appraises capital investment projects using a 10% cost of capital.

(a) Complete the table below and calculate the net present value of the proposed replacement machine (to the nearest £000). Use a minus sign to indicate a negative figure. Enter 0 where any figure is zero.

	Year 0 £000	Year 1 £000	Year 2 £000	Year 3 £000
Capital expenditure				
Disposal				
Sales revenue				
Operating costs				
Net cash flows				
PV factors	1.0000	0.9091	0.8264	0.7513
Discounted cash flows				
Net present value				

Tick to show if the net present value is

positive	
negative	

or

The directors of Clark Ltd have a major project they are planning to undertake.

The following information relating to the project is available:

- at a cost of capital of 10%, the project gives a positive net present value of £95,800

- at a cost of capital of 20%, the project gives a negative net present value (ie net present cost) of £18,200

(b) Calculate, using interpolation, the internal rate of return of the project (to the nearest percentage).

Practice assessment 3

This Practice Assessment contains ten tasks and you should attempt to complete every task.
Each task is independent. You will not need to refer to your answers to previous tasks.
Read every task carefully to make sure you understand what is required.

Where the date is relevant, it is given in the task data.
Both minus signs and brackets can be used to indicate negative numbers unless task instructions say otherwise.

You must use a full stop to indicate a decimal point. For example, write 100.57 NOT 100,57 or 100 57
You may use a comma to indicate a number in the thousands, but you don't have to. For example, 10000 and 10,000 are both acceptable.

Task 1

Crosskeys Ltd uses raw material CK55 in the manufacture of its products. The company had the following quantities of CK55 in inventory:

Date purchased	Quantity (kg)	Cost per kilo £	Total cost £
5 October	5,000	5.00	25,000
10 October	2,500	5.08	12,700
24 October	3,500	5.10	17,850

From the following amounts, insert the correct cost into the cost column of the table below to record the issue of 7,000kg of CK55 on 25 October and to record the inventory balance after the issue using:

- FIFO (first in, first out)
- AVCO (weighted average cost)

Amounts:

£20,000   £35,160

£20,400   £35,350

£20,200   £35,550

£20,390   £35,700

	Cost
FIFO issue	
AVCO issue	
FIFO balance	
AVCO balance	

Task 2

In December, Crosskeys Ltd made a number of transactions which must be accounted for using the journal
The following account codes are relevant.

Code	Account name
1118	Grade CK18 metal
1378	Component CK378
2003	CK3 work-in-progress
3000	Bank
5250	Purchase ledger control

(a) Identify the correct entries in the journal to record the transaction by writing the appropriate options in the relevant boxes, and inserting the correct amounts (correct to two decimal places).

Receipt of 8kg Grade CK18 metal into inventory as a cash purchase at £22/kg.

	Account code	Account name	Amount £
Debit			
Credit			

Options for (a):

1118, 1378, 2003, 3000, 5250

Bank, Purchase ledger control, Grade CK18 metal, CK3 work-in-progress, Component CK378

(b) Identify the correct entries in the journal to record the transaction by writing the appropriate options in the relevant boxes, and inserting the correct amounts (correct to two decimal places).

Issue of 19 units of type Component CK378 (cost £550 per 40 units) to production CK3.

	Account code	Account name	Amount £
Debit			
Credit			

Options for (b):

1118, 1378, 2003, 3000, 5250

Bank, Purchase ledger control, Grade CK18 metal, CK3 work-in-progress, Component CK378

(c) Three units of Component CK378 were not used in production of 'CK3 work-in-progress' and were returned to inventory.

Complete the following sentence by selecting the appropriate item:

To account for this, account 2003 should be CREDITED / DEBITED and account 1378 should

be CREDITED / DEBITED .

Task 3

Crosskeys Ltd pays its employees on a weekly basis. All employees are required to complete a weekly timesheet which is then used to calculate the gross pay due. Basic pay is calculated as total hours worked multiplied by the basic rate.

Complete the timesheet below using the data given. (**Note:** Overtime premium is just the premium paid for the extra hours worked. Your figures should be entered to two decimal places. If no hours are due then you must enter a zero figure in the relevant table cell.)

The timesheet is for T. Hall, an employee in the Machining Department, for the week ended 28 November. Employees in the Machining Department are paid as follows:

- For a basic six-hour shift every day from Monday to Friday, and three hours on a Saturday – £12 per hour.

- For any overtime in excess of the six hours on any day from Monday to Friday – additional hours are paid at basic pay plus an overtime premium equal to half of basic pay (time and a half).

- For any overtime in excess of the three contracted hours on a Saturday – the additional hours are paid at basic pay plus an overtime premium equal to basic pay (double time).

- Any hours worked on Sunday are paid at basic pay plus an overtime premium equal to basic pay (double time).

Employee:	T. Hall		Profit Centre: Machining			
Employee number:	CK041		Basic pay per hour: £12.00			
	Hours spent on production	**Hours worked on indirect work**	**Notes**	**Basic pay £**	**Overtime premium £**	**Total pay £**
Monday	7					
Tuesday	6	2	2pm-4pm first aid course			
Wednesday	6					
Thursday	8					
Friday	8	1	8am-9am maintenance			
Saturday	4					
Sunday		2	inventory checking			
Total	39	5				

Task 4

Crosskeys Ltd has the following information for its two profit centres and three support cost centres:

Budgeted overheads	£	£
Depreciation charge for machinery		45,800
Power for production		36,300
Rent and rates of premises		36,000
Light and heat for premises		15,600
Indirect labour costs:		
Maintenance	40,310	
Stores	22,196	
General administration	51,422	
Totals	113,928	133,700

Additional information				
Department	Carrying amount of machinery £	Machinery power usage (KwH)	Floor space (square metres)	Number of employees
Profit centres:				
Machining	250,400	14,632	1,200	7
Finishing	121,600	8,968	900	4
Support department cost centres:				
Maintenance			120	2
Stores			80	1
General administration			100	3
Total	380,000	23,600	2,400	17

Overheads are allocated or apportioned on the most appropriate basis. The total overheads of the support departments' cost centres are then reapportioned to the two profit centres in the following way:

* 50% of the Maintenance cost centre's time is spent maintaining production machinery in the Machining profit centre, 30% in the Finishing profit centre and the remainder in the General administration department.

* The Stores cost centre makes 75% of its issues to the Machining profit centre, and 25% to the Finishing profit centre.

* General administration supports the two profit centres equally.

Use the table below to allocate or apportion the budgeted overheads using the most appropriate basis.

Indicate negative figures with minus signs, NOT brackets.

Select your entries for the 'Basis of apportionment' column from the following list: Allocated, Carrying amount of machinery, Floor space, Number of employees, Production machinery power usage.

Budgeted overheads	Basis of apportionment	Machining £	Finishing £	Maintenance £	Stores £	General admin £	Totals £
Depreciation charge for machinery							
Power for production							
Rent and rates of premises							
Light and heat for premises							
Indirect labour							
Totals							
Reapportion Maintenance							
Reapportion Stores							
Reapportion General admin							
Total overheads to profit centres							

Task 5

Crosskeys Ltd has the following information for its Machining and Finishing departments:

Quarter 1	Machining	Finishing
Budgeted direct labour hours	1,385	1,320
Budgeted machine hours	2,650	750
Actual direct labour hours	1,430	1,450
Actual machine hours	2,750	810
Budgeted overheads	£38,425	£24,750
Actual overheads	£41,250	£26,550

(a) The budgeted overhead absorption rate (to two decimal places) for the Machining department based upon machine hours, and for the Finishing department based upon labour hours, is:

	Machining £	Finishing £
Budgeted overhead absorption rate	per hour	per hour

(b) Complete the following sentence by selecting the appropriate item and inserting the correct amount:

In Quarter 1 overheads for the Machining department were

OVER-ABSORBED / UNDER-ABSORBED

by £ [   ]

(c) In Quarter 2, if the overhead absorption rate for the Finishing department is £19 per labour hour, the actual overheads incurred were £26,550 and the actual labour hours used were 1,450, complete the following table:

	Overheads incurred £	Overheads absorbed £	Difference absorbed £	Under/over absorption £
Finishing department				

Task 6

Crosskeys Ltd has prepared a budget for the next month for one of its products, CK45. The budget is based on producing and selling 600 batches.

One of Crosskeys Ltd's customers has indicated that it may be significantly increasing its order level for product CK45, so it now appears that activity levels of 900 batches and 1,350 batches are feasible.

The fixed costs are fixed within a production range of up to 1,499 batches. Above that level extra indirect labour costs will be incurred.

(1) Complete the table below and calculate the budgeted profit per batch of CK45 at the different activity levels.

CK45 batches produced and sold	600	900	1,350
	£	£	£
Sales revenue	5,100		
Variable costs:			
• Direct materials	1,320		
• Direct labour	1,080		
• Overheads	540		
Fixed costs:			
• Indirect labour	300		
• Overheads	600		
Total cost	3,840		
Total profit	1,260		
Profit per batch (to 2 decimal places)	2.10		

Crosskeys Ltd estimates that if it produced 1,500 batches of CK45 there will be extra fixed costs of £450.

(2)   Complete the following sentences by selecting the appropriate item and inserting an amount (correct to two decimal places).

The profit per batch of CK45 increases with increasing activity levels up to 1,499 batches because:

fixed costs per batch decrease	
fixed costs per batch increase	
variable costs per batch decrease	
variable costs per batch increase	

At a production level of 1,500 batches the extra fixed costs will cause the profit per batch to

DECREASE / INCREASE

by £ [   ]

(3)   As an accounting technician, you are working on the accounts of a vehicle repair business. The owner tells you that she wishes to use either marginal costing or absorption costing – "whichever will show the higher profit as I need to impress the bank manager".

How do you respond to this?

(a)	It is unethical for an accounting technician to manipulate profits in this way	
(b)	A good idea – let's see if we can think of further ways to increase profits	
(c)	I'll need to tell my supervisor that we are doing this	
(d)	I'll do it if, in return, one of your employees can repair my car	

Task 7

(a)   Choose the correct description for each of the three terms in the table below.

Select your entries for the 'Description' column from the following list:
   Selling price plus variable costs
   Sales volume where there is neither profit nor loss
   Selling price less total costs
   Excess of actual sales over breakeven sales
   Set amount of profit above breakeven
   Profit when selling price equals variable costs
   Excess of breakeven sales over actual sales
   Sales revenue where there is neither profit nor loss
   Contribution divided by selling price
   Selling price less variable costs

Term	Description
P/V ratio	
Target profit	
Margin of safety	

Crosskeys Ltd has prepared annual budgeted information for two of its products, CK70 and CK90.

Product	CK70	CK90	Total
Units sold	15,000	12,000	27,000
Sales revenue (£)	90,000	66,000	156,000
Direct materials (£)	40,500	22,200	62,700
Direct labour (£)	28,500	17,400	45,900
Variable overheads	6,000	3,600	9,600
Fixed overheads (£)	15,000	11,000	26,000

(b) Complete the table below (to two decimal places) to show the budgeted contribution per unit of CK70 and CK90 sold, and the company's budgeted profit or loss for the year from these two products.

	CK70 £	CK90 £	Total £
Selling price per unit			
Less: variable costs per unit			
Direct material			
Direct labour			
Variable overheads			
Contribution per unit			
Sales volume (units)			
Total contribution			
Less: fixed overheads			26,000
Budgeted profit/loss*			

*delete as appropriate

The total cost of producing 4,500 units of CK99 has been calculated as £27,000 and of producing 6,000 units is £29,625. The only increase in cost is the increased volume of production.

(c) Complete the following sentence by entering the appropriate figure (to two decimal places).

The fixed cost of producing CK99 is £ _____

and the variable cost of producing one unit of CK99 is £ _____

Task 8

Crosskeys Ltd is to begin producing a new metal component as from 1 January. It will be using process costing to account for the manufacture of this new component.

The component requires the input of three different materials:

- Material A: 150 kilograms @ £15.00 per kilogram
- Material B: 250 kilograms @ £20.00 per kilogram
- Material C: 100 kilograms @ £50.00 per kilogram

(a) Complete the table below (to two decimal places) to show the total cost of the materials input into the process.

Materials	£
Material A	
Material B	
Material C	
Total	

Crosskeys estimates that the process will require four operatives to work 20 hours each. These operatives will be paid an hourly rate of £12.50.

Overheads are to be absorbed on the basis of £20 per direct labour hour.

(b) Calculate the total labour cost and total overhead cost for the manufacture of the new metal component, to two decimal places, and complete the sentence below.

The total labour cost for the manufacture of the new metal component is £ ⬚

The total overhead cost for the manufacture of the new metal component is £ ⬚

(c) Calculate the total quantity and value of inputs into the process for the new metal component, to two decimal places, and complete the sentence below.

The total quantity of materials input into the process is ⬚ kilograms

and the total value of inputs into the process is £ ⬚

Crosskeys expects 10% of the input to be scrapped during the manufacturing process. The scrap can be sold at £4.50 per kilogram.

(d)   Calculate the total scrap value of the normal loss of 10% of input. Your answer must be stated to two decimal places.

The total scrap value of the normal loss of 10% of input is £ [   ]

(e)   Calculate the cost per kilogram of output assuming a normal loss of 10% of input. Your answer must be stated to four decimal places.

The cost per kilogram of output assuming a normal loss of 10% of input is £ [   ]

(f)   Complete the sentences below, to identify the appropriate accounting entries. Enter your answer for amounts to two decimal places.

If the process results in an output of 440 kilograms there will be:

An abnormal gain	
An abnormal loss	
A normal gain	
A normal loss	

of [   ] kilograms.

This will have a total value of £ [   ].

Task 9

Crosskeys Ltd budgeted to manufacture 8,000 units of product CK85 last quarter. However, due to an increase in demand it was able to manufacture and sell 10,000 units.

(1)   Complete the table below to show a flexed budget and the resulting variances against this budget for the quarter. Show the actual variance amount, for sales revenue and each cost, in the column headed 'Variance'.

Note:

•   Adverse variances must be denoted with a minus sign or brackets.

•   Enter 0 where any figure is zero.

	Original budget	Flexed budget	Actual	Variance
Units sold	8,000	10,000	10,000	
	£	£	£	£
Sales revenue	100,000		122,500	
Less costs:				
Direct materials and direct labour	42,300		51,750	
Variable overheads	21,500		26,325	
Fixed overheads	22,000		22,500	
Profit from operations	14,200		21,925	

(2)   Referring to your answer for part (1), which **one** of the following has had the greatest impact in decreasing profit from operations?

(a) Sales revenue	
(b) Direct materials	
(c) Direct labour	
(d) Fixed overheads	

(3) Which **one** of the following might have caused the variance for direct materials and direct labour costs?

(a) An increase in employees' pay	
(b) An increase in material prices	
(c) Less efficient use of direct labour	
(d) A decrease in material prices	

Task 10

Crosskeys Ltd is considering a possible capital investment project.

It will base its decision upon using three appraisal methods, the results of which are shown below:

Appraisal method	Notes	Company policy	Project results
Payback period		3 years	4 years
Net present Value (NPV)	Discount at 12% cost of capital	Accept if positive	+£24,000
Internal Rate of Return (IRR)	Discount at 12% cost of capital	Must exceed cost of capital	15%

The company considers Net Present Value to be the most important investment criteria.

Identify the correct recommendation for each decision in the table below.

Select your entries for the 'Recommendation' column from the following list:

Accept as positive

Reject as more than 3 years

Reject as negative

Accept as more than 3 years

Reject as per most important investment criteria

Accept as greater than the cost of capital

Reject as lower than the cost of capital

Accept as per most important investment criteria

Appraisal method	Recommendation
Payback period	
NPV	
IRR	
Overall	

Answers to practice assessment 1

Task 1

	Cost
FIFO issue	£1,965
AVCO issue	£2,016
FIFO balance	£1,185
AVCO balance	£1,134

Task 2

Transaction	Account debited	Account credited	Amount £
1 Paid wages of direct labour employees. 270 hours at £14 per hour.	Production direct costs	Wages control	3,780
2 Paid wages of factory supervisors. Basic pay £2,200 + £150 overtime.	Operating overheads	Wages control	2,350
3 Paid wages of stores department staff. £1,050 + 10% bonus.	Operating overheads	Wages control	1,155
4 Paid wages of general administration department staff. £1,760 + 20% bonus.	Non-operating overheads	Wages control	2,112

Task 3

(a)

Labour cost	Hours	£
Basic pay	210	2,940
Overtime rate 1	20	350
Overtime rate 2	30	630
Total cost before team bonus	260	3,920
Bonus payment		700
Total cost including team bonus		4,620

(b)   The total labour cost per unit for June is **£0.84**

(c)   The basic pay and overtime for each member of team 8 for June was **£1,960** and the bonus payable to each team member was **£350**.

Task 4

Budgeted overheads	Basis of apportionment	Cutting £	Finishing £	Maintenance £	Stores £	Admin £	Totals £
Depreciation charge for machinery	Carrying amount of machinery	2,670	1,780				4,450
Power for production	Production machinery power usage	2,376	594				2,970
Rent and rates of premises	Floor space	3,325	2,375	665	1,140	1,045	8,550
Light and heat for premises	Floor space	875	625	175	300	275	2,250
Indirect labour	Allocated			16,400	30,300	35,650	82,350
Totals		9,246	5,374	17,240	31,740	36,970	100,570
Reapportion Maintenance		8,620	6,896	−17,240		1,724	
Reapportion Stores		22,218	9,522		−31,740		
Reapportion Administration		19,347	19,347			−38,694	
Total overheads to profit centres		59,431	41,139				100,570

Task 5

(a) Cutting £9 per hour; finishing £10 per hour

(b) Cutting £14 per hour; finishing £11 per hour

(c) Cutting under-absorbed £400; finishing over-absorbed £600

Task 6

(a)   **£1.07** (£6,400 + £4,300) ÷ 10,000 units

(b)   **£1.60** (£17,200 − £1,200) ÷ 10,000 units

(c)   **£1.33** (£6,400 + £4,300 + £2,600) ÷ 10,000 units

(d)   **£10,700** £6,400 + £4,300

(e)   **£16,000** £17,200 − £1,200

(f)   (a)   Product costs

(g)   (b)   Treating Westlake's profit as confidential

(h)   (c)   To report segmented profits or losses

(i)   (b)   The costs of support centres used by the Production Department are apportioned to it

Task 7

(a)

Term	Description
Breakeven units	Sales volume where there is neither profit nor loss
Margin of safety	Excess of actual sales over breakeven sales
Target profit	Set amount of profit above breakeven

(b)   220 units

(c)   £5,280

(d)

Units of WL15 sold	400	500
Margin of safety (units)	180	280
Margin of safety (percentage)	45	56

(e)   520 units

Task 8

Cost	Description
Fixed cost	Option 5
Variable cost	Option 1
Semi-variable cost	Option 6
Stepped cost	Option 7

Task 9

(1)

	Original budget	Flexed budget	Actual	Variance
Units sold	3,000	3,240	3,240	
	£	£	£	£
Sales revenue	19,500	21,060	22,100	1,040
Less costs:				
Direct materials	5,500	5,940	5,800	140
Direct labour	4,300	4,644	4,900	−256
Fixed overheads	6,700	6,700	7,100	−400
Profit from operations	3,000	3,766	4,300	524

(2) (a) Sales revenue

(3) (d) An increase in employees' pay

Task 10

(a)

	Year 0 £000	Year 1 £000	Year 2 £000	Year 3 £000
Capital expenditure	−40			
Disposal				6
Sales revenue		33	40	35
Operating costs		−12	−15	−14
Net cash flows	−40	21	25	27
PV factors	1.0000	0.9091	0.8264	0.7513
Discounted cash flows	−40	19	21	20
Net present value	20			

or

positive	✔
negative	

(b)   The payback period is 1 year and 10 months (rounded up to the next month).

Answers to practice assessment 2

Task 1

(a) EOQ = 75 kg

Tutorial note:

$$\sqrt{\frac{2 \times 1,125 \times 25}{10}}$$

(b) and (c)

Inventory record for plastic grade CL5

Date	Receipts			Issues			Balance	
	Quantity (kg)	Cost per kg £	Total Cost £	Quantity (kg)	Cost per kg £	Total Cost £	Quantity (kg)	Total Cost £
Balance as at 22 December							40	170
24 December	75	4.40	330				115	500
28 December				85	4.329	368	30	132
29 December	75	4.60	345				105	477
30 December				55	4.491	247	50	230

Workings:

24 December:	40 kg at £4.25 = £170 + 75 kg at £4.40 = £330, total 115 kg = £500
28 December:	40 kg at £4.25 + 45 kg at £4.40, total 85 kg = £368
29 December:	30 kg at £4.40 = £132 + 75 kg at £4.60 = £345, total 105 kg = £477
30 December:	30 kg at £4.40 + 25 kg at £4.60, total 55 kg = £247

Task 2

Date	Code		Dr £	Cr £
7 December	5501	Plastic cutting direct costs	5,040	
7 December	9000	Wages control account		5,040
8 December	5502	Plastic assembly direct costs	4,500	
8 December	9000	Wages control account		4,500
10 December	6000	Operating overheads	1,760	
10 December	9000	Wages control account		1,760
11 December	7000	Non-operating overheads	2,530	
11 December	9000	Wages control account		2,530

Task 3

	Cost £	
Calculation **(a)**	**1,960**	140 hours x £14
Calculation **(b)**	**84**	12 hours x £7 premium
Calculation **(c)**	**420**	15 hours x £28
Calculation **(d)**	**2,632**	1,960 + (£168 + £84) + £420

Task 4

(a)

Overhead	Basis of apportionment
Depreciation of cutting equipment	Carrying amount of cutting equipment
Rent and rates of production departments	Factory floor space
Quality control costs	Number of quality control inspections
Assembly equipment maintenance costs	Time spent servicing assembly equipment
Assembly equipment insurance costs	Carrying amount of assembly equipment

(b)

Budgeted overheads	Cutting £	Assembly £	Maintenance £	Stores £	Admin £	Totals £
Depreciation of equipment	3,500	2,500	800	200	500	7,500
Power for production	1,920	1,280				3,200
Rent and rates of premises	3,520	2,640	1,320	440	880	8,800
Light and heat for premises	1,520	1,140	570	190	380	3,800
Indirect labour costs	12,000	16,000	26,200	38,360	49,140	141,700
Administration costs					2,650	2,650
Totals	22,460	23,560	28,890	39,190	53,550	167,650
Reapportion Administration	21,420	21,420	5,355	5,355	−53,550	
Reapportion Stores	26,727	17,818		−44,545		
Reapportion Maintenance	27,396	6,849	−34,245			
Total overheads to profit centres	98,003	69,647				167,650

(c)   The fixed element of the machine running costs that will be apportioned to the Cutting profit centre is **£20,196**

The variable element of the machine running costs that will be apportioned to the Assembly profit centre is **£6,318**

Task 5

(a)

	Cutting £	Assembly £
Budgeted overhead absorption rate	23.75 per hour	16.50 per hour

(b) In Quarter 1 overheads for the Assembly department were **OVER-ABSORBED** by **£475**

(c)

	Overheads incurred £	Overheads absorbed £	Difference absorbed £	Under/over absorption
Cutting department	27,230	27,000	230	under-absorption

Task 6

(a) **£1.76** (£6,240 + £4,320) ÷ 6,000 units

(b) **£2.48** (£15,930 – £1,050) ÷ 6,000 units

(c) **£1.99** (£6,240 + £4,320 + £1,360) ÷ 6,000 units

(d) **£10,560** £6,240 + £4,320

(e) **£14,880** £15,930 – £1,050

(f) (b) Period costs

(g) (c) Using Twitter to disclose Clark's profits to friends

(h) (c) To report segmented profits or losses

(i) (a) The Production Department is responsible for its total costs and revenues

Task 7

(a)

Term	Description
Contribution	Selling price less variable costs
Limiting factor	Scarce resource which restricts output
Breakeven revenue	Sales revenue where there is neither profit nor loss

(b)   400 units

(c)   £6,000

(d)

Units of CL18 sold	500	800
Margin of safety (units)	100	400
Margin of safety (percentage)	20	50

(e)   550 units

Task 8

(a)

Process Account							
Description	kg	Unit cost £	Total cost £	Description	kg	Unit cost £	Total cost £
Material CL54	140	3.50	490	Normal loss	12	3.00	36
Material CL75	40	5.00	200	Output	228	13.00	2,964
Material CL96	60	4.50	270				
Labour			1,496				
Overheads			544				
	240		3,000		240		3,000

(b)

	Debit	Credit
Abnormal gain	✔	
Transfer to next process		✔

Task 9

(1)

	Original budget	Flexed budget	Actual	Variance
Units sold	2,500	2,250	2,250	
	£	£	£	£
Sales revenue	30,200	27,180	27,310	130
Less costs:				
Direct materials and direct labour	10,600	9,540	9,440	100
Variable overheads	6,900	6,210	6,460	−250
Fixed overheads	5,100	5,100	5,620	−220
Profit from operations	7,300	6,030	5,790	−240

(2) (c) Variable overheads

(3) (c) An increase in the selling price

Task 10

(a)

	Year 0 £000	Year 1 £000	Year 2 £000	Year 3 £000
Capital expenditure	−40			
Disposal				8
Sales revenue		25	30	34
Operating costs		−10	−12	−15
Net cash flows	−40	15	18	27
PV factors	1.0000	0.9091	0.8264	0.7513
Discounted cash flows	−40	14	15	20
Net present value	9			

positive	✔
or
negative	

(b)

$$10\% \quad + \quad \left[\frac{£95,800}{£114,000} \quad × \quad 10 \right] \quad = \quad 18.4\% \text{ or } 18\% \text{ (to the nearest whole percentage)}$$

Answers to practice assessment 3

Task 1

	Cost
FIFO issue	£35,160
AVCO issue	£35,350
FIFO balance	£20,390
AVCO balance	£20,200

Task 2

(a)

	Account code	Account name	Amount £
Debit	1118	Grade CK18 metal	176
Credit	3000	Bank	176

(b)

	Account code	Account name	Amount £
Debit	2003	CK3 work-in-progress	261.25
Credit	1378	Component CK378	261.25

(c)   Account 2003 should be **CREDITED** and account 1378 should be **DEBITED**.

Task 3

	Hours spent on production	Hours worked on indirect work	Notes	Basic pay £	Overtime premium £	Total pay £
Employee: T. Hall			Profit Centre: Machining			
Employee number: CK041			Basic pay per hour: £12.00			
Monday	7			84	6	90
Tuesday	6	2	2pm-4pm first aid course	96	12	108
Wednesday	6			72	0	72
Thursday	8			96	12	108
Friday	8	1	8am-9am maintenance	108	18	126
Saturday	4			48	12	60
Sunday		2	inventory checking	24	24	48
Total	39	5		528	84	612

Task 4

	Basis of apportionment	Machining £	Finishing £	Maintenance £	Stores £	General admin £	Totals £
Depreciation charge for machinery	Carrying amount of machinery	31,144	14,656				45,800
Power for production	Prod'n machinery power usage	22,506	13,794				36,300
Rent and rates of premises	Floor space	18,000	13,500	1,800	1,200	1,500	36,000
Light and heat for premises	Floor space	7,800	5,850	780	520	650	15,600
Indirect labour	Allocated			40,310	22,196	51,422	113,928
Totals		79,450	47,800	42,890	23,916	53,572	247,628
Reapportion Maintenance		21,445	12,867	−42,890		8,578	
Reapportion Stores		17,937	5,979		−23,916		
Reapportion General admin		31,075	31,075			−62,150	
Total overheads to profit centres		149,907	97,721				247,628

Task 5

(a)

	Machining £	Finishing £
Budgeted overhead absorption rate	14.50 per hour	18.75 per hour

(b) In Quarter 1 overheads for the Machining department were **UNDER-ABSORBED** by **£1,375**

(c)

	Overheads incurred £	Overheads absorbed £	Difference absorbed £	Under/over absorption
Finishing department	26,550	27,550	1,000	over-absorption

Task 6

(1)

CK45 batches produced and sold	600	900	1,350
	£	£	£
Sales revenue	5,100	7,650	11,475
Variable costs:			
• Direct materials	1,320	1,980	2,970
• Direct labour	1,080	1,620	2,430
• Overheads	540	810	1,215
Fixed costs:			
• Indirect labour	300	300	300
• Overheads	600	600	600
Total cost	3,840	5,310	7,515
Total profit	1,260	2,340	3,960
Profit per batch (to 2 decimal places)	2.10	2.60	2.93

(2) The profit per batch of CK45 increases with increasing activity levels up to 1,499 batches because: fixed costs per batch decrease.

At a production level of 1,500 batches the extra fixed costs will cause the profit per batch to **DECREASE** by **£0.30**

(3)   (a)   It is unethical for an accounting technician to manipulate profits in this way

Task 7

(a)

Term	Description
P/V ratio	Contribution divided by selling price
Target profit	Set amount of profit above breakeven
Margin of safety	Excess of actual sales over breakeven sales

(b)

	CK70 £	CK90 £	Total £
Selling price per unit	6.00	5.50	
Less: variable costs per unit			
Direct material	2.70	1.85	
Direct labour	1.90	1.45	
Variable overheads	0.40	0.30	
Contribution per unit	1.00	1.90	
Sales volume (units)	15,000	12,000	
Total contribution	15,000	22,800	37,800
Less: fixed overheads			26,000
Budgeted **profit**			11,800

(c)   The fixed cost of producing CK99 is **£19,125**

and the variable cost of producing one unit of CK99 is **£1.75**

Task 8

(a)

Materials	£
Material A	2,250.00
Material B	5,000.00
Material C	5,000.00
Total	12,250.00

(b)   The total labour cost for the manufacture of the new metal component is **£1,000.00**
The total overhead cost for the manufacture of the new metal component is **£1,600.00**

(c)   The total quantity of materials input into the process is **500 kilograms**
and the total value of inputs into the process is **£14,850.00**

(d)   The total scrap value of the normal loss of 10% of input is **£225.00**

(e)   The cost per kilogram of output assuming a normal loss of 10% of input is **£32.5000**

(f)   If the process results in an output of 440 kilograms there will be an **abnormal loss** of **10 kilograms**.
This will have a total value of **£325.00**.

Task 9

(1)

	Original budget	Flexed budget	Actual	Variance
Units sold	8,000	10,000	10,000	
	£	£	£	£
Sales revenue	100,000	125,000	122,500	–2,500
Less costs:				
Direct materials and direct labour	42,300	52,875	51,750	1,125
Variable overheads	21,500	26,875	26,325	550
Fixed overheads	22,000	22,000	22,500	–500
Profit from operations	14,200	23,250	21,925	–1,325

(2)   (a)   Sales revenue

(3)   (d)   A decrease in material prices

Task 10

Appraisal method	Recommendation
Payback period	Reject as more than 3 years
NPV	Accept as positive
IRR	Accept as greater than the cost of capital
Overall	Accept as per most important investment criteria